Historic Wells In and Around Bradford

Covering:
Bradford Metropolitan area,
parts of Leeds,
Kirklees,
Calderdale and
North Yorkshire

Val Shepherd
with drawings and photographs
by the author

Heart of Albion Press

**Historic Wells
In and Around Bradford**

ISBN 1 872883 31 1

Printed in England by
DAR Printing 0664 424785

Heart of Albion Press
2 Cross Hill Close, Wymeswold,
Loughborough, LE12 6UJ

This book is dedicated to
Stanley my husband.

Acknowledgements:-

The author wishes to thank those who have helped her to produce this work. Mr R J Duckett, Senior Librarian, Bradford Libraries, Helen Gomersall of West Yorkshire Archaeology Service, Wakefield, Bradford Countryside Service, the late Ernest Davies, Mrs White and Alex Robinson of Idle and Thackley Heritage Group, Dorothy Burrows, Mr and Mrs Osbourne, Bryan Whitfield, Tony Hegginbotham, Ian Mason, Senior Archivist, West Yorkshire Archive Service, and *Bradford Telegraph and Argus* 'library', Peter Rayner, Paul Bennett, John Billingsley, Arthur Edwick, Stella Carpenter, J. Holden Luscombe, Susan Stead, Albert Shutt, Mr and Mrs Unwin, Mrs Ashton, Julia Smith, Michael Wilcox and Brian Larkman. Special thanks go to Edna Whelan (whose book *Yorkshire Holy Wells and Springs* was the inspiration for the present work) and to Bob Trubshaw of Heart of Albion Press.

For permission to reproduce maps and photographs:-

Town and Township of Bradford 1802, Bradford Libraries.
Lady Well Estate 1849, Bradford Libraries.
Holywell Ash Estate, West Yorkshire Archive Service, Bradford.
Burnwells, Mary Heggs and Idle and Thackley Heritage Group.
Town Wells Cottingley, Dorothy Burrows.
Loin Spout, Baildon, Norman Entwhistle and Arthur Edwick,
Countryside Publications
Rawsons map of Halifax 1842, Halifax Reference Library.
Drinking fountain, White Wells; Carved stone spout and Eastern Bath; and Water Cure, David Carpenter and Smith Settle.
Map of Ailsa Well in 1852, Dorothy Burrows.
Stone head, Prince of Wales park, Bingley, Susan Stead

Contents:-

Introduction 1

Wells of Bradford City centre 4

Wells of Fairweather Green, Manningham,
Heaton 11

Wells of the outer villages:
Bingley, Shipley, Eccleshill, Idle, Wibsey, Clayton, Cockham,
Great Horton, Queensbury, Thornton, Allerton, Cullingworth,
Harecroft, Cottingley, Baildon, Wilsden, Harden 16

Wells further out:
Howorth, Laycock, Keighley, Hawksworth, Guiseley,
Menston, Pudsey, Wyke, East Bierley, Drighlington,
Hartshead, Roberttown, Drub 49

Wells of Halifax:
Priestley Green, Halifax, Northowram 67

Wells of Ilkley, Ilkley Moor, Addingham 72

Wells of other areas:
Denton, Otley, Oxenhope, Adel, Yeadon, Rawdon 86

Other lost wells 89

Ley line 92

Glossary 93

References and bibliography 95

Index 100

Note: North is at the top of all maps unless shown otherwise.

Imperial measurements are used throughout.

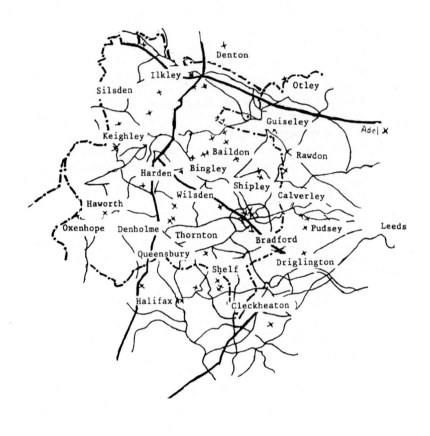

Location of wells   ✗

Roman roads

(and supposed Roman roads)

Modern roads

Bradford Metropolitan boundary   — ˙ — — ˙ — ˙ —

General area covered by text

Introduction

What is a well? On first thought one may think that is an unnecessary question, as everyone knows what a well is. In my researches on this subject, I have found that the word does indeed need to be defined as there can be misunderstandings.

Any flowing water, especially a small spring issuing out of a hillside or bubbling up from the ground, is by its use a water supply, called a well. Many such wells were altered by fitting a stone basin into which the water flowed for the convenience of collecting it in containers. Some wells in towns and villages were fitted with a hand pump. Draw wells were man-made shafts lined with stone or brick, to tap the water table. Artesian wells were created by certain geological conditions in which deep water can be forced to the surface naturally or by drilling. Draw wells or artesian wells were sometime built into a structure with a pitched roof and a winding apparatus to lower a bucket into the water. This type of design has become a romantic stereotype. These different types of well were, and are, the most commonly found.

Many wells date from prehistoric, Celtic and Roman times, while others date from the early Christian era. In prechristian times they were considered to be places where the 'Earth Spirit' resided, symbolic of life and fertility so any spring where the life giving waters of Mother Earth came out of the ground was not only respected but the 'residing spirit' worshipped and the spot made 'holy'.

Rivers and all water features were venerated. The river Wharfe was associated with the Goddess 'Verbeia', the guardian of the river in Roman times. When the Norse people arrived, they brought their own traditions and dedicated wells to 'Thor'. A Thor's Well still exists in the parish of Burnsall. 'Our Lady's Well' or 'Lady Well' was a popular dedication in Christian times. Old pagan names were Christianised as a compromise measure; as well worship was so strong a custom the early Christians could not stamp it out, and very soon, folk customs, religious practices and superstitions became intermingled. There were regional differences, as in present day well dressing customs in Derbyshire; and up to the 19th century rag wells were common in some areas, while in Yorkshire bent pins were offered at pin wells. Wishing wells and wells used for divination were common. Many wells were used to heal one particular ailment such as Sore Eyes Well in Shipley Glen. The more important holy wells had attendants who took money. Those wells would often have been totally enclosed within a stone building with an entrance door. A drinking cup was often attached to the well by a metal chain. Such a well lies in Calverley Woods. One of the most important characteristics of a holy well was that it never dried up (unless the supply was tampered with).

Some wells of the healing kind were chalybeate (pronounced 'kal-i-be-at'), that is, containing iron. Such wells were of special medicinal value and it became fashionable to create spas (e.g. Ilkley and Harrogate) where people could 'take the waters' by drinking and bathing. The waters were piped through different outlets, some of which were in the form of a carved head (still surviving at Adel and White Wells).

Many cattle troughs were constructed which cannot always be separately identified as such. Some may have served both man and beast. More elaborate drinking fountains were constructed in the 19th century, some combining with cattle troughs, having troughs or basins at different levels. Some fountains (which can be classed as wells also) were connected with the Temperance movement, as is the one in Prince of Wales Park, Bingley.

It is not possible to consider old wells, especially holy wells, in isolation. A water source, being a focal point for people to gather around, led to the construction of settlements or other marks of the human hand, so we have those remnants from the past: standing stones, earthworks, Roman roads, ancient trackways, churches, boundaries, sacred trees and remnant placenames. All can be associated with an original water source. Folklore too, has arisen at the sites, as there are many tales of ghosts and fairies which are said to haunt wells.

Trees growing by water soak up a tremendous amount of that water so it can be said that if the water is holy then the tree can impart the divine qualities of the water to the people beneath. This is the reason why certain trees were planted near wells, especially on the south side where the tree could impart its beneficial shadow over the well. Ash is the tree most frequently found next to wells in Yorkshire. In Norse legend an ash was the World Tree, Yggdrasil, and in Anglo-Saxon times there was a written reference in 854AD by a Christian priest to an ash tree 'as one which the ignorant call holy'. Hawthorn, rowan and elder are also deeply embedded in British folklore and are found often at wells.

Stone collects water in its cavities and stones near wells could have been carved to hold water. This water was charged with the qualities of the stone and was used for healing, initiation and baptism. Such stones are found near wells, usually in the form of 'Wart Stones', one of which stood at 'Holy Well

2

Ash', Manningham. Stone troughs made to contain the well water could have added healing properties to the water.

Many of the well rituals still survive in Ireland and give us conformation of such practices at England's wells.

The West Yorkshire Archaeology Service have records of holy wells which were in existence in the period 400 to 617AD, some of which are included in this work. There is less official evidence of other wells having a holy background but remnants of folk memories picked up by mainly 19th century local historians give strong clues in that direction. I refer often to them.

The use and veneration of wells has declined so much that many wells have been lost. Generally they are not valued as our ancestors valued them. We do not need to go to a well for our water supply any more or to rely on holy water for healing, but then, we spend money buying spring water from sources in Britain and the Continent or fill up bottles at moorland springs. Clearly there is an interest in water quality and this needs to be nurtured in the direction of our local wells. The wells are part of our history and when a well is lost or dries up it is a loss of our heritage.

Of wells still running, it must be stated that no-one should drink the water unless they know that it is fit to drink. It is a sad reflection of our day that this should be so. Many pollutants from industry, farms and domestic sources can and do seep into wells. Some springs do provide drinking water but they are tested regularly. There is a need to clean up the supply if we wish to drink the water with confidence. In some areas this is being done and people take pride in their local water, but one should be wary. Some wells are on private land where permission to visit a well needs to be obtained from the owner.

Science has confirmed what the ancients knew instinctively that moving water contains beneficial ions and that due to the mineral contents and low bacteria content of some wells, they do indeed have health giving properties. Sensitive people can also detect 'something else' which makes such places 'special'; something not just in the water but in the natural surroundings, especially at a beauty spot.

In the Bradford area there were at least three important holy wells and about ten in other areas which I have included in this publication. Healing wells, 'pin' and 'rag' wells and wells which the 'Guytrash' used to haunt are all mentioned. Some wells which have been destroyed have a fascinating history put together from many different sources.

The geographical area includes the Bradford Metropolitan Area and parts of Leeds, Kirklees, Calderdale and North Yorkshire. The total area covers about half of West Yorkshire.

Wells of Central Bradford

BOAR'S WELL

Grid Ref SE1645 3435

Bradford

I begin with this well because it is the one most connected with the City of Bradford. The story of the killing of the last wild boar is well recorded. It was in the 14th century that a ferocious boar was said to frighten people who lived in the area where it roamed. The king himself offered a reward to anyone who succeeded in killing it. It was killed by a man who cut out its tongue as evidence because he could not carry away the whole animal. Another man found the boar, cut off its head and presented it at court to claim his prize, but the first man came forward with the tongue and was duly rewarded. When a coat of arms was granted to Bradford the head of the wild boar was depicted above the shield, minus its tongue and a symbol of the well on the shield. There is also a Viking legend in which the boar is sacred to Freya, the Earth Goddess; a legend which may have come to Yorkshire with the Vikings and become attached to the well. The boar was also the emblem of St Antony who has wells dedicated to him; one of which is in Harden and another in Northowram.

In medieval times Boar's Well, which is a natural spring, was in the middle of a large wood, Cliff Wood, on Bradford Bank which stretches from the parish church (now cathedral) to Shipley and beyond. The wood was used for timber, the grazing of pigs and cattle and for many industrial uses. In the 17th century plague victims were buried there and by the 20th century most of the trees had gone and it became a dumping ground for stone waste from the quarries above along with other rubbish.

At the present time the area is being given a new lease of life and the whole hillside is now designated an Urban Wildlife Reserve and should eventually look near to how it

Bradford Coat-of-Arms

may have looked when the wild boar roamed there, and we will be able to drink at the spring where the boar drank. The spring has been renovated and made into an attractive little waterfall with a pool beneath. Credit is due to Bradford Metropolitan Council and the Bradford Urban Wildlife Group.

Boar's well

SPINKWELL

Grid Ref SE1653 3410
Bradford

About 200 yards south of Boar's Well is a little spring, Spinkwell, which was of great note for long periods. It provided water of spa quality that was channelled into a purpose-built bath house for patients who came to 'take the waters', as at any other spa. In 1788, Spinkwell House, located below the spring, was advertising its cold baths and bowling green. Gravestones remembering plague victims of 1645 were built into its walls. The graves were found when Peel Park (SE175345) was being made. The bathers did not know then that the building was to become a 'lunatic asylum'. All the associated buildings have now been demolished leaving only the spring above, which is being restored. The area abounds with Spinkwell placenames, 'spink' meaning 'chaffinch', a bird of the woodlands.

JACOB'S WELL

Grid Ref SE1635 3279
Bradford

This well is about 200 years old and started out as a well in the cellar of a cottage, one of a row. The owner of the cottage sold the well water for 1d a bucket and became known locally.

Wells were mentioned frequently in connection with Jacob in the Old Testament but why this well is called Jacob's Well I do not know, unless the original owner was called Jacob.

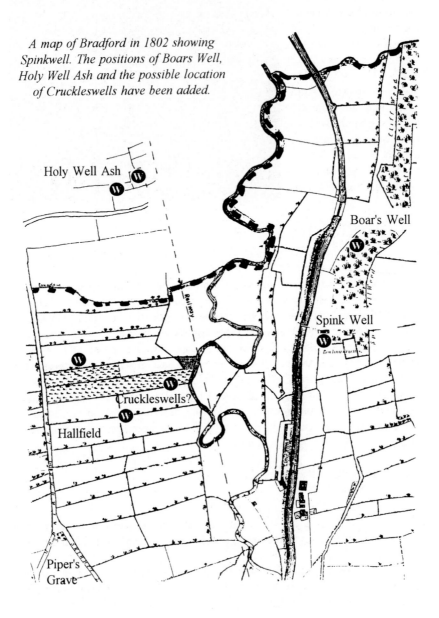

A map of Bradford in 1802 showing Spinkwell. The positions of Boars Well, Holy Well Ash and the possible location of Cruckleswells have been added.

Holy Well Ash

Boar's Well

Spink Well

Cruckleswells?

Hallfield

Piper's Grave

The cottage became one of the oldest public houses still in existence in Bradford although the date of the change of use is not known. In 1964 all the old property around it was demolished leaving the pub isolated. The well was covered over with concrete at that time. The well water, still under cover, keeps the beer cool in the cellar. The pub, named of ourse Jacob's Well, gave its name to the area including the modern council offices next to the building.

RANDALL WELL

Grid Ref SE159 329
Bradford

This well was near to what is now Randall Well Street in the centre of Bradford. The well, which was described as a draw well, 'sprang up in the midst of a small wood above Bradford Beck' in an area which had 'rural charms' in the 18th century (James' *The history of Bradford*). Until 1820 people met there to gossip and the 'maidens of Bradford resorted to it to obtain tea water' and washed themselves in it to gain a healthy skin. Pilgrims also visited on certain days. It was mentioned in the days of Elizabeth I as being in Randall Well Close and by 1665 was part of James Sagar's charity lands. An octagonal chapel was built nearby in 1766 but it was so badly constructed that it had to be demolished about 70 years later.

In 1802 Randall Well Close was described as belonging to the trustees of Thornton Chapel and was rented by Mr Whitaker, a brewer. The brewery was situated east of the well site. In the middle of the 17th century James Ellis of Thornton had a plan to pipe the water to Bradford Cross at the top of Ivegate, for the convenience of the population. He also planned piping water from Cruckleswells. He created a trust to execute his plan, just before his death, but it was not carried out. After 1820 the estate owner sold the Close and when a Mr Fawcett bought Holme Mill (which was on the north western side of the beck) he put in a pipe from the well so that the neighbours, after crossing the beck by plank, obtained a never failing supply of water. John James said that in 1841 the well was 'covered over by a portion of the engineering works of Mr Thwaite'. The Alexandra Hotel

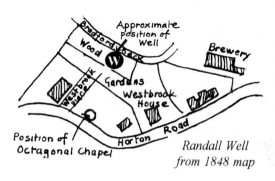

Randall Well from 1848 map

occupied most of the Close until 1993 and the well site must be beneath the car park at the rear. A walled embankment defines the northern edge of the site below which the beck lies, culverted.

SCHOOLHOUSE WELL

Grid Ref SE1600 3323

Bradford

This gives its name to Well Street in the city centre and was 'a fine spring of water which supplies that end of town near the Grammar School and Hoppy Bridge over the beck'. Hoppy Bridge was named after Henry Hoppy, an usher at the Grammar School, who lived at the White House, which locals called Hoppy House in the 18th century. He organised a charity for the poor, collecting the money which was known as 'Hoppy Money'. The old Grammar

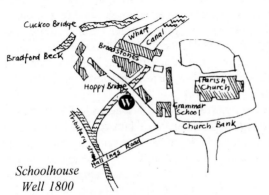

Schoolhouse Well 1800

School was situated at the west side of the parish church. Well Street crossed Hoppy Bridge and the well was beside it, four steps down, surrounded by willows. The site became a coach builder's premises in 1866 and now the area is under the island in Forster Square.

CRUCKLESWELL(S)

Grid Ref SE162338 approx

Bradford

These wells (three marked on the first edition OS map of 1847) were described as being in a close of the same name 'between Manningham Stoop [at Carr Syke near Bradford Grammar School] and Hallfield Cross [near Hallfield House, Manningham Lane]'. 'Cruckle' meant 'bent or crooked pin', an item of good luck. These pins were made as votive offerings at wells in return for healing or when making a wish. The wells were first described in 1664. (Sources: Renton [no date; c.1900] and Robertshaw 1934.)

8

In the 17th century James Ellis of Thornton planned to pipe the water to Bradford Cross (top of Ivegate) but his plan fell through (see Randall Well and the map on page 6).

LADY'S WELL

Grid Ref
SE1691 3220
Ripleyville, Bowling

A holy well of medieval origin, this is the 'Lady's Well in the Roughs on the west side of Dudley Hill', as described by Ogden and James in their histories of Bradford. The description is rather misleading as the site is nowhere near Dudley Hill but nearer to Bradford city centre at the corner of Hall Lane and Mill Lane.

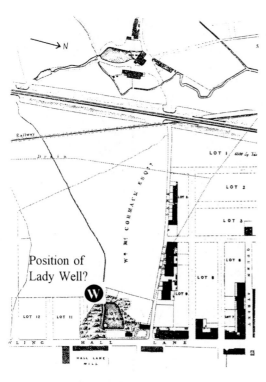

Map of Lady Well Estate 1842

The site became Lady Well Pit, a coal mine from which a 'sough' drained away water into Bowling Beck. In 1849 it was within a small estate still called Lady Well. A sale map of the time shows two buildings and a huge 'fish pond' surrounded by rough ground, the scale of the pond being out of proportion to the estate. There is a stream leading from the well which presumably is on the western side (see map).

In 1853 Benjamen Berry built a textile machinery works on the site and used the well.

In 1926 Bradford Corporation decided to make the area on the western side into an unof-

9

ficial 'park'. They made a children's padding pool and named it 'Lady Well Park' after the well. The water from the well would have been channelled to make the paddling pool (SE1688 3222). The water also ran into a dam within the mill. The mill still exists and a computer firm has a building on Lady Well Park. The mill dam was filled in several years ago and the water source had probably dried up. The site was approximately 200 yards from the Roman road into Bradford from Drighlington. People were said to visit the well up to the 1840s but the coal mine must have existed before that date; it may have been a small 'bell pit' type.

BOLLING HALL WELLS
Grid Ref SE173 314
Bradford

Bolling Hall may have existed on this site in some form at least since the time of William the Conqueror. The Roman road into Bradford lies about 200 yards to the east. A ley line may connect it with Bradford Cathedral (that may reflect the tunnel legend connecting the two sites). The oldest part of the present building is the Pele tower built in about 1340 and soon after that date the two draw wells were constructed, one on each side of the Hall. They are 30 ft deep and still contain water.

Originally the Hall was surrounded by a moat. The estate was well wooded and later formed a deer park. The Hall and the family of Bolling has had a long history and today the Hall is a museum of great interest. The adjoining Bowling Park was made out of part of the deer park.

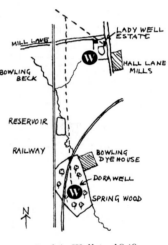

Lady's Well in 1849

KIRK WELL (or DORA WELL)
Grid Ref SE1685 3160
Bowling

This well supplied soft water to the mills of Bowling in the last century. The mill owners relied on it so much that when there was a plan to build a railway line from Low Moor to the city centre and beyond there was great concern that the well would be disturbed. The plan may not have affected the well but the project did not materialise. From the information it is likely that the well was in Spring Wood, south of Bowling Dyeworks. The wood had disappeared by 1891. The area houses a chemical works and the water runs into reservoirs but recent environmental improvements have encouraged nature to return.

TEA WELL,
BATH WELL,
WORKHOUSE WELL

Grid Ref SE148 346 approx
Horton

These wells were in the area which was to become Horton Park. There was a workhouse there which was demolished in 1822 and replaced by Wellclose House. Mr Noble, the owner, planted many trees on his estate and built a bath house over the Cold Spring. Previously the paupers were bathed in the Workhouse Well, with or without their consent is not told. Horton Park was opened in 1878 and advantage was taken of the watercourses for making ornamental lakes and streams. The Park took over the 12 acres which belonged to Wellclose House and the cricket field was made from the 17 acres of Low Close Farm and 14 acres bought from other owners.

HOLY WELLS near Crossley Hall

Grid Ref SE1305 3330
Fairweather Green, Bradford

The Knights Hospitalers held the Manor of Crossley. Before 1258 a deed of Byland Abbey refers to Crossley Hall, describing the boundaries which include Brokewell Rode, Caldwell Syket and Bysksby (Birks). Pontefract Priory also had possessions there and referred to a road at Hallewell. There is a well marked near Birks and another between Crossley Hall and Shuttleworth Hall on the first edition OS map. A holy well was said to be between Cemetery Bridge and Crossley Hall. (Bell 1882; James 1866).

Speight, in *Pleasant Walks Around Bradford* (1890), suggests that Spa Beck Public Gardens were in the vicinity of Bull Greave Wood (potentially a lovely spot). The position of the spa is not identified but a well-worn paved path across the fields, with stone stiles, runs from Scholemoor to Crossley Hall. Could the spa have been one of the holy wells? The two halls have been demolished and the area built up on the north side of Middle Brook, which becomes Bradford Beck.

ASHWELL

Grid Ref SE1415 3433

Toller Lane, Manningham.

This well, now lost, is likely to have been an early holy well because on the Manningham tithe map and field list appear the field names Penwell or Pinwell suggest it existed in that area. In a survey of 1611 Saxton drew a map of the large common fields of Manningham and included the area bounded by Toller Lane, Duckworth Lane, Allerton Road and Whetley Lane, called the 'Panwell Feilde', the north-western part being the actual field. In a Manningham tythe map of 1850 there is a field called 'Pen Well' and below it 'Little Pen Well'. 'Penwell Close' is marked on other maps and situated where Ashwell House was, now the position of St Chad's Church. Pen Well was not built upon until the 19th century when Manningham Thorpe was built (now Lillycroft Working Men's Club). The position of the well would be at the entrance drive, the road being widened at that point in the 1880s. The Roman road which ran through Bradford would pass within a few yards.

The name change to 'Ashwell' must have occurred in the 18th or early 19th centuries. It gave its name to Ashwell Road and Ashwell Street. Speight in *Pleasant Walks Around Bradford* writes that there used to be a 'fine railed off ash tree opposite Oakwood Villas' and there are other ash trees around the area today. This is not to say that the ash was always associated with the well.

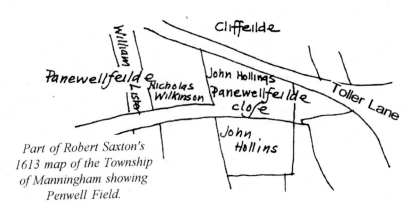

Part of Robert Saxton's 1613 map of the Township of Manningham showing Penwell Field.

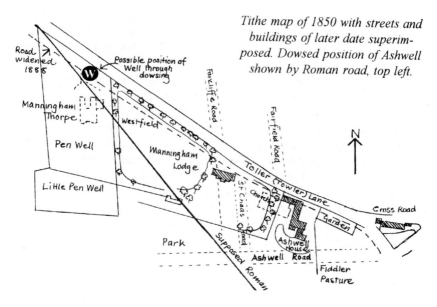

Tithe map of 1850 with streets and buildings of later date superimposed. Dowsed position of Ashwell shown by Roman road, top left.

HOLYWELL ASH

Grid Ref SE1600 3420

Manningham

This well was the most famous in 18th century Bradford and for centuries before. It is alluded to in many documents and maps produced by various historians. In the 18th century people came to drink the waters on Sundays and holidays (or holy days) and to meet their friends. 'It was a fine old well, covered over and preserved with great care. It had a great ash tree over it and a standing stone next to it called the Wart Stone. It was a healing stone itself. Pins, coins, rags and food were left as offerings to appease the Spirit of the Place'.

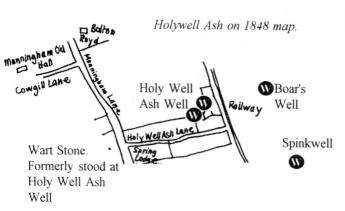

Holywell Ash on 1848 map.

By the beginning of the 19th century its popularity had declined and those who looked after the well had to resort to bringing sulphur spa water from Harrogate, charging ½d per cup! By the 1880s it was built upon but then became a quarry in the late 19th century before being filled and turned into Manningham football ground. This ground is now the home of Bradford City Football Club. In its day the well was approached from Manningham Lane by 'Holy Well Ash Lane' which still exists in its lower half. The 'Wart Stone' also known as the 'Pin Stone' was built into the wall (the date this was done is unknown) and, later, transferred to a position on Manningham Lane opposite the top of Holy Well Ash Lane. It was still there in 1911, but where is it now?

There were two other wells near to the Holy Well. I have no information about them but they are shown on the OS map as having trees around them. The water was piped to a reservoir a few yards away, the structure of which was still apparent at the side of the railway line until recently. These wells are now under Midland Road.

ASHWELL

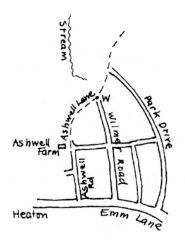

Grid Ref SE1435 3582

Heaton

Now lost, this well was on an old path, Ashwell Lane, between Heaton and Frizinghall. It is probably under tarmac at the junction of Wilmer Drive and private drives to new housing. A stream which runs from the gardens of the houses runs down through Renold Wood to Seans Pond making a strong possibility that the water still runs from the well underground. It gave its name to Ashwell Farm, the lane and the road.

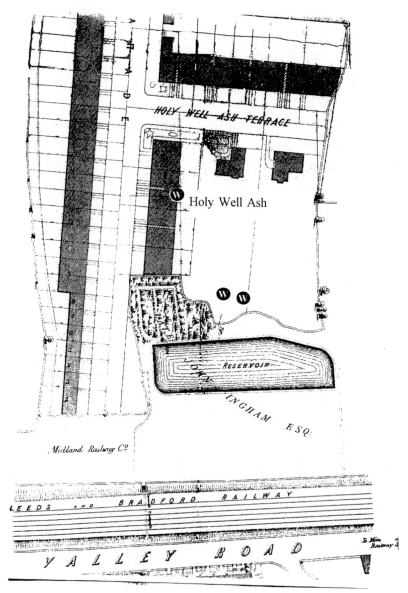

Part of Holy Well Ash estate 1871.
Courtesy West Yorkshire Archives Service Ref. 1D78/54

15

BINGLEY

WATERING WELL

Grid Ref SE107 391

Bingley

This well gave its name to Watering Well Hill and Watering Well Steps, near the river behind Airedale Street and the Arts Centre. It is now lost but provided Bingley with water at one time. Nearby Sharpe's mill (SE1065 3910) was demolished in the 1960s together with the streets around it, used to pump water from the river by a donkey engine, the donkey being made to walk around a central shaft to operate a pump. The water was directed to a huge circular container and then pumped to a dam at Prospect Mill in Chapel Lane, also owned by Sharpe's.

There may or may not be a connection here with the original well. The river bank is about to be improved and named 'Watering Well Riverwalk'.

AILSA WELL

Grid Ref SE1058 3931

Bingley

Oral tradition connects this well with a saint so it is likely to have been a holy well. All we have in writing is from the 19th century via Speight and Turner. Then the well was named (or renamed) after Alice Hird, a 'wise' woman who lived in a fisherman's cottage near the well. Ailshirds is another variation of the name. The fisherman who used to live there, perhaps in the 18th century, was a woolcomber by trade but made more money catching trout and grayling in the river and selling it at Bingley market which was situated at the top of nearby Ferrands Lane. The ginnel can be seen on the map. There was an ancient route across the river by stepping stones

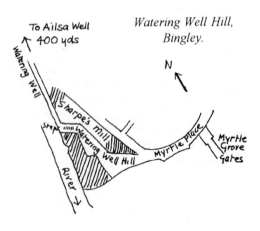

To Ailsa Well
↑ 400 yds

Watering Well Hill,
Bingley.

N ↑

from the bottom of Ferrands Lane.

The well had hard water, ice cold and was renowned for healing sprains and for cooking vegetables. At one time the area around the well was public land which also contained the public oven. There was a ginnel leading to the well from the river bank public path.

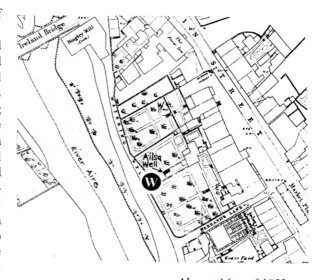

Above: *Map of 1852 showing Ailsa Well at the end of a ginnel. Another well marked to north.*
Below: *Ailsa well in about 1970. Not to scale.*

It has been neglected for at least 70 years and almost buried in rubble until 1993. There are trees in the area today but the position in the rear yard of shops is not ideal.

It has now been restored, thanks to the owner and to the late Ernest Davies, historian, who almost single-handedly cleared the well of tons of silt and rubbish. A plaque will be placed near the well in his memory as part of a general improvement of the riverside that is taking place.

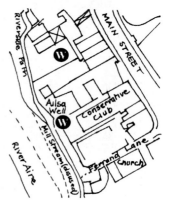

The well itself consists of a stone-lined rectangular well house with a stone slab roof. Six steps lead down to a platform in front of a smooth carved trough into which an angled stone spout directs a copious flow of clear water (though, after testing, the well was declared polluted). Small carved holes in the floor and at the back of the trough direct the overflowing water underground a short distance to the river. The design of the stonework may be 18th century or earlier. The well was never known to run dry.

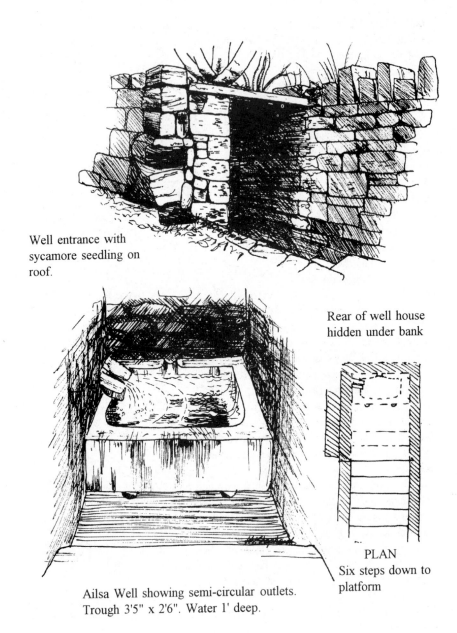

Well entrance with sycamore seedling on roof.

Rear of well house hidden under bank

Ailsa Well showing semi-circular outlets. Trough 3'5" x 2'6". Water 1' deep.

PLAN
Six steps down to platform

A grid has been put over the trough to prevent people from drinking the water, which I hope is a temporary measure and the source of the pollution can be cleared.

Ailsa is a Scottish girls' name, probably a corruption of Gaelic Ealasiad (Elizabeth). Ailsa Craig, the rocky island off the west coast of Scotland, has a Nordic connection derived from 'Alfsigesey' i.e. Island of Alfsigir, elf and victory. Also, in Norse legends the Alaisigae are goddesses or spirits connected with Odin. Could Ailsa or Ailshirds Well have its origins in Nordic times and been dedicated to the goddesses? It may have been a coincidence that the wise woman of the well who looked after it in the 18th or 19th century, Alice Hird, had a similar name. The name of the saint still eludes detection. My thanks to Michael Wilcox for help with attempting to trace the name of this well.

SPA WELL

Grid Ref SE1121 4005

Bingley

This well lies on Spa Lane where there is an elaborate stone drinking fountain set into a wall. It was built by Thomas Garnet, the owner of Oakwood Hall through whose estate the stream runs which supplied the well. He made a lake in his grounds but now this is a stream once more, running through the

Spa Well, Spa Lane, Bingley.

19

Above: *Stone head from Spa Well*
Photograph coiurtesy of Susan Stead
Right: *Prince of Wales Park, Bingley.*

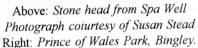

gardens of modern houses. The water is not now connected up to the fountain but flows underneath, then below a footbridge, to form a ford (not for modern traffic). There is a hawthorn bush nearby and the lane is well wooded. Speight says that the water was renowned and beautifully clear, an excellent tonic as it was slightly chalybeate. It was very popular in Victorian times.

In the nearby Prince of Wales Park (SE 116403) Speight says that there were 'copious springs' which were 'known for their great purity and coldness resembling the Ilkley Wells'. Two of the wells are on the north side of the park (SE1150 1030) consisting of large stone troughs. One trough supplies a garden pond and the other, higher up, supplies water for cattle over the field. The park was made in 1863 and was previously called Brown Hill, perhaps a corruption of the Celtic *bron*, meaning 'a hill slope'. It is the site of a post-Roman 'entrenchment'. A stone head was found near there some years ago and is cemented into a stone hut there.

Brown Hill Well (SE1155 4010) issued from the south side of the park and may have been piped to a Victorian drinking fountain near the main entrance. This has the inscription 'Pure Water Be Mine 1866. Presented by the Total Abstainers of Bingley'. It is now dry and in a dilapidated condition.

20

FAIRY WELL
Grid Ref SE1378 3954
Gilstead

Now built over, fairies were said to be seen at this well, and 'in olden times locals would visit it to drink the healing waters and leave rags called "memaws" tied to the trees' (P. Bennett, *pers. comm.*) and left pins also as votive offerings. There was a 'fairies hole' in a nearby rock. The well was contained within a trough with railings around it, and it was marked on the first edition OS map. More recently a waterboard cover was put over it.

PRIESTTHORPE SPRING
Grid Ref SE1128 3955
Bingley

The Priestthorpe district was the site of a Norse settlement but now an urban part of Bingley. The spring was later incorporated into a dry stone wall at the junction of Priestthorpe Road and Crownest Road adjoining the garden of Priory Garth. It is a simple stone basin fed by an ugly pipe, with a grate for the outflow, but is now dry. Tradition tells of its use for brewing tea.

JANET'S WELL OR JENNET'S WELL
Grid Ref SE1115 3947
Bingley

This is a short distance below Priestthorpe spring at the side of Priestthorpe Road issuing from underneath the road and forming a stream in a private garden . It is at the corner of an old stone wall with the remains of metal railings around a stone slab which is propped up. An elder tree overhangs and wild flowers grow there - it would be a romantic spot were it not for the adjoining electricity station.

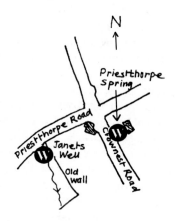

Janet's Well and Priestthorpe Spring, Bingley. After a map of 1889.

ELM CRAG WELL or BELL BANK WELL

Grid Ref SE1028 3910

Bingley

This well is above Bingley just off the road to St Ives and beautifully situated in Bell Bank Wood. There is a huge boulder beneath which is a small grotto from which the water flows. Ferns, lichen and water plants grow in and around this grotto. A few centuries ago Killarny fern was discovered here by Dr Richardson. Later in the 18th century two other botanists found it, one of whom found the grotto or cavern destroyed. This cavern was probably behind the present outlet. Water authorities have made full use of this spring to supply Bingley in the past including the brewery of the Brown Cow Inn. . There used to be a connecting trough on the main road. Today there are a few courses of ugly brick partially built across the natural outlet of the spring which seems to serve no purpose now. The water is clear and pleasant.

'Bel' of Bell Bank Wood may have originated with the Goidelic Celts who used to inhabit the area and perhaps, therefore, used this spring.

OUR LADY'S WELL

Grid Ref SE1141

Bingley

The position of this well is unknown but it was said to be in the fields to the west of Lady House (SE113405) or Lady House Farm which was to become the site of Bingley Training College. It gave its name to Lady Lane. Lady House was an ancient property of the 'Chantry of Our Lady'. At the Reformation the property was transferred to Bingley Grammar School. There is a stream running at the back of the old training college, now flats, which opens out into a pleasant pond. This stream almost certainly is the one which flows to Spa Well on Spa Lane. There used to be a trough of iron water by the side of Lady lane at a point where the stream goes under the road. At the other side it flowed into a pond in the grounds of Oakwood Hall but now flows through the gardens of new houses.

WELLS ON THWAITES BROW AND MARLEY BROW

Grid Ref SE077408 to 091406

Bingley

This is on the south side of the Aire near Bingley where there are some very ancient homesteads and farms with numerous springs and wells. This beautiful hillside has extensive views of the Aire Valley although now intruded upon by the new road below. There is an old trackway from Bingley to Marley via Raven Royd. Marley was mentioned in the Domesday Book and its Hall is the second known building on the site. Its well on the hillside above (SE 0911 4054) was a disappointing sight when visited and was only running at a trickle. At Blackey House (SE 0900 4070) the trough outside the entrance is dry and overgrown, while at Jackfield Farm the chalybeate Spa Well is situated behind the barn (SE 0804 4080) and was used for the water supply until recently. There is another iron-looking spring at Currer Laithe (SE0819 4050) and at Royd Field Farm (SE0772 4070) by the public footpath is a spectactular iron spring. An old boundary lies to the west and a Roman road lies to the east of Jackfield Farm.

According to Speight the 'old British trackway through Hollins was used for funerals from the high moors.' This track goes within yards of Druids Altar and climbs the hill to join the Roman road near Jack-fields.

Chalybeate spring near Royd Field Farm

GOFF WELL

Grid Ref SE0620 3870

Keighley

High on a hill, south-east of Keighley is Goff Well Farm, on Goff Well Lane. It is said by Speight that 'Goff' may mean 'red' and could have been connected with a red haired hermit who lived nearby. The well was 'dressed' in times past and was a resort of gypsies before the moor was enclosed in 1861. The site, in a field near the farm, is known but not accessible.

DRUIDS WELL

Grid Ref SE0940 3980

Bingley

Below Druids Altar in an area of wild romantic grandeur, of which local writers made full use in the 18th and 19th century. They could visualise the

ancient Britons walking the old trackways towards their circular huts at their settlement of Bailey Hills, the earliest settlement in Bingley. On the heights of Druids Altar they could visualise the Druids worshipping the rising or setting sun, lighting their Beltane fires and offering sacrifices on the rock, the blood from which was gathered in the carved cup mark in the stone from where it overflowed into a channel. They could imagine them gathering oak branches, cut-

Druid's Well

ting the mistletoe with a golden sickle and drinking the pure waters of the well below.

Sydney Greenbank was one such author, though writing in the 1920s, whose 'fancy' ran free but his imagination and speculation can give clues where hard facts are few. He tells us of the well and his finds; 'Lower down the craggy slopes almost hidden by overgrown grasses, a spring of crystal water gushes out of the brown soil; this is always spoken of as Druids Well, - the author finding at this spot, after a casual surface scratching, a flint scraper, several flakes and a large polished flint bead slightly bored at both ends - probably formed one of a bangle or neclace. May be it was a love token and mayhap this spring was a trysting place'. The author also said, in a footnote, that Mr W Packman of Crossflatts as a youth found a long knife made of bronze and curved like a new moon, at the foot of Druids Altar.

The surroundings of the well are still wild and secluded and the well itself is still a natural spring which flows from the base of a huge boulder. Its floor is sandy and its waters have a beautiful sweet taste. Immediately above grow a mature birch and ash.

The finding of such artefacts described confirms the long association of man with this area and a possible real Druidic connection cannot be ruled out.

Shipley Glen Wells

Loadpit Beck runs down this attractive well-wooded glen which forms the boundary of Bingley and Baildon. A series of springs are found, all named. From north to south they are: Sore Eyes Well, Judson Well, Raygate Well, Wood Well, Crag Well and Nursery Well. An ancient iron smelting site lies near to Sore Eyes Well and there are many 'cup and ring stones' on the nearby moor. A fault line runs along the glen and strange lights have been seen there travelling along the glen (Devereux 1990). Two stone circles lie on the shelf immediately above the glen.

SORE EYES WELL
Grid Ref SE1284 4012
Shipley Glen

This was a rag well, a holy well where people made offerings of rags for the benefits given to them by the water. It was situated on a wooded bank near a rowan tree. A sewage overflow pipe is situated very near to the well or has taken over the well site. On a rocky outcrop to the south are large cup marks.

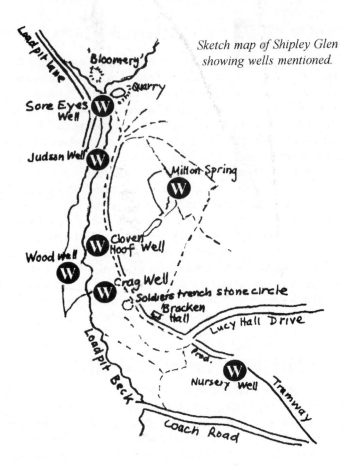

Sketch map of Shipley Glen showing wells mentioned.

JUDSON WELL

Grid Ref SE1290 3980

Shipley Glen

This spring now has an insignificant flow of water that issues beneath an old silver birch.

RAYGATE or CLOVEN HOOF WELL

Grid Ref SE1286 3936

Shipley Glen

A beautiful spring with large boulders nearby, one of which is impressed with the resemblance of a cloven hoof, hence the name.

26

Raygate or Cloven Hoof Well.

WOOD WELL
Grid Ref SE1280 3920
Shipley Glen
This spring, on the west side of the glen, now has an insignificant flow.

CRAG WELL
Grid Ref SE1288 3914
Shipley Glen
This is an attractive natural spring at the bottom of the glen. It seeps out of rocks which are overhung with ferns.

NURSERY WELL
Grid Ref SE1355 3870
Shipley Glen
This well is a natural spring issuing below the old fairground but extremely overgrown and just identifiable by the large boulders around it.. It was said to be a place where children were brought to be cured of childhood ailments in the 17th century. A large ash stood over the well but now sycamores dominate (Paul Bennett, *pers. comm.*)

LOW WELL

Grid Ref SE151377

Shipley

This well served an old part of Shipley that is now demolished. A huge bank of earth covers the site, near the railway station.

WELL CROFT

Grid Ref SE1465 3720

Shipley

Hall Lane, a narrow country lane in the last century leading to the Manor House and the Over Hall, was where the well was described by Cudworth in *Round about Bradford..* In 1679 it was spoken of as being remarkable for the purity of its water. 'Well Croft' was a field name east of the later 'Well Croft Mills'. The position of that field now is behind the police station. The present 'Wellcroft' street name is quite a distance from the original well.

SWEET WILLY WELL

Grid Ref SE1666 3645

Wrose

This well lies at the bottom of a recreation field on the boundary between Idle and Wrose, also on a footpath. The water comes out of a stone-lined cavity. A slow trickle of clean looking water issues from it and flows a very short distance through a bluebell-carpeted little valley, but then the valley becomes a rubbish tip where a rat and a robin share the same patch. A spoil tip from Bolton Woods quarry overlooks the site and a sewer overflow joins the stream which then disappears underground. I imagine it would have been a pretty spot in the last century with many more trees than its present sparse representation of hawthorn, elder and sycamore. A case here for improvement.

The present stream is known as Trap Sike, but was called Linwell Sike in the past. Cudworth (*History of Bolton in Bradford Dale*) described it as being between North Spring Wood and South Spring Wood with a road 24 ft wide running from north to south, to the Towns Well (which may have been this well).

HOLY WELL

Grid Ref SE188362

Eccleshill

This well has a fascinating history. The name Eccleshill may be derived from an ancient sacred site, *eccles* being Old English for 'church'. A chapel may have existed next to the holy well. Holy Acres and Chapel Flatts nearby are place-names giving added clues. On the earliest OS map of 1847 the well is shown to be at the end of Holy Well Grove covered with trees, leading up the hill. There were no houses immediately around then.

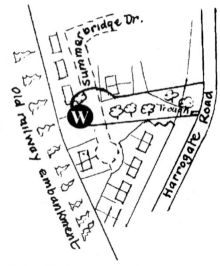

Holywell Grove, Eccleshill with modern roads and buildings superimposed.

In 1585 there was a deed which allowed the local people to take water from the well, a right which was forgotten or abused, for in 1723 the well was inaccessible. In 1737 there was a drought and the well was the only water in the area. This resulted in a court case in which the people were given access once more. Previously John Stanhope, the owner, had to bring a claim against one woman for diverting it in 1704. The Stanhopes built Eccleshill Hall in 1773 and the estate, in which the well was at the eastern end, made into a deer park. In the 19th century the estate was divided up and in 1851 the 'Holy Grove' was the property of Bradford Corporation, the well being still 'a bathing place', but later it was 'neglected, full of weeds, and a few old trees stood by'. The railway, adjoining the site, was built in 1854, the embankment looking down onto the site (Preston, *Bradford Antiquary*).

Today houses have been built in the cul-de-sac of Summerbridge Drive but a snicket from the main road lies along the line of the Grove, and has large trees, one of them being an ash. The well may be still running under a garden, as water floods out into the main road after heavy rain.

In another part of the village, near the old Manor Pottery was the Wart Stone. Whether it had any connection with the holy well or whether it was moved is not known.

Idle

The village of Idle has a long history. At one time it consisted of two hamlets, Idle at the top and Thorpe at the bottom of the hill. Many springs came through from Idle Moor in the west and the inhabitants channelled the water to supply troughs. The main troughs were at Town Gate, Town Well and the well on the green. The wells do not appear to have distinctive names, apart from one, and may have had more than one name at different times.

In 1853 there was a *General Board of Health Report on Idle* in which the water quality of the wells was described. The water quality described ranged from 'good' to 'indifferent' and 'dry for half the year'. No mention was made of any medicinal quality of a well. However in Wright Watson's *Idlethorpe,* informs us that James Booth, who built Thorpe House (Thorpe being considered a better class suburb of Idle in the 17th century) put an advertisement in the *Leeds Intelligence* in 1772. It reads:

WILLIAM a ROYD'S WELL

Mr James Booth takes this method of acquainting the Public that there is in his estate in the township of Idle near Apperly Bridge, a fine spring of clear water whose Virtues are not inferior to that at Ilkley for the curing of all Scrofulus Humours, Running Sores, Sore Eyes etcetera; and he hath made a very commodious 'Bathing Well' with a House and Court adjoining.. As the air of the town is remarkably fine and healthy, and convenient accomodation may easily be procured, he is in Hopes his Labours will not be unacceptable to the Public.

Wright Watson also states 'the water which supplied William Royd's Well ran through the garden of Thorpe House and still runs through the garden of Thorpe Cottage' (this is in 1950) and 'in 1775 Butt Lane Mills were built. There was an agreement for safeguarding the Well Spring and the right to draw water from it. From the spring a stream ran down through Dye House Croft into the fold where there were horse steps and a water trough for cattle. The stream still runs from Well Spring, through Mill Fold, but now it makes its way under the Mill into the Union Dam, then flows underground, under Butt Lane and New Street to the new Mill Dam . . . Mr Thompson had a school in a house close to the Causer or Causeway Well near to where the railway bridge spans the High Street'.

From this scanty and sometimes confusing information I have compiled a description of the Idle Wells.

TOWN WELL (Upper)

Grid Ref SE1769 3792

Idle

This well consisted of trough with a pump, fitted with a gas lamp on top (as seen in an early photograph). It was next to the Old Chapel, a chapel of ease at Town Gate. The present Old Chapel is the second building on the site, built in 1630. A school known as the Round Steps School was built onto the west side of the Chapel in 1750. The village stocks were here too. Overshadowing the area was a large elm tree which also was surrounded by stone steps, around which people gathered as a general meeting place and for political meetings. The elm was removed in the 1860s and the well was capped, the site being made into an empty well house although the well is marked on old maps. The 'White Bear' and the 'New Inn' overlook the site.

TOWN WELL (Lower) also called LOW WELL

Grid Ref SE1778 3788

Idle

This well stood outside the Old Manor House, half way down the High Street. This house was described as 'declining' in 1584. There was so much change of ownership, rebuilding, extensions and partitioning off, that it is surprising that there are still substantial 17th century houses around the site at Garth Fold and High Street Place. Part of the Manor House was made into the Manor House Inn and an inn next to the pinfold adjoining the well was called Town Well. The pinfold was removed in 1869 and the well site is in an open paved area on a side road in front of a private house. What form the well took is not recorded. The area was haunted by the 'Guytrash' or 'Gabbleratchets' (see Glossary).

WELL opposite the Alexandra Inn

Grid Ref SE1802 3782

Idle

This well was at the lower end of Thorpe Garth near the Smithy. It took the form of a trough which was fenced. It was probably fed from the well at the top of Thorpe Garth (which may have been the Well Spring). The water from the well then ran down Howgate to the Union Mill pond. It does not exist now.

WELL SPRING

Grid Ref SE1788 3745

Idle

The name seems appropriate for this well as it was near Wells House and Garth House, old houses which were demolished in the 1960s. In the 1893 map it is shown as a trough on the road side.

WILLIAM a ROYD'S WELL

Grid Ref SE1810 3750

Idle

William a Royd, as described by James Booth, was probably William Roddes who lived in a cottage and held a barn and garth in Idle in 1584 (*Bradford Antiquary* 1880). If that is so, James Booth would have been right in claiming that the well on his premises was William's well and tried to make use of it (see above). I have not found a record of whether the spa was a success.

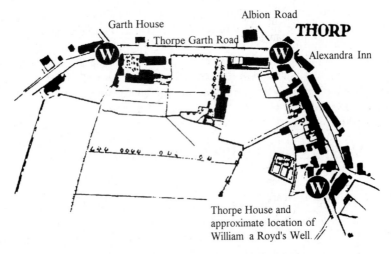

Map of Thorp about 1870 showing the two wells on Thorp Garth Road and the site of William a Royd's Well at Thorpe House.

NOOKING WELL

Grid Ref SE1786 3760

Idle

This well stood at the end of a ginnel near where an old outbuilding still stands on Bradford Road. An old bollard stands near. The well gave its name to the 'Nook Inn'. The 'Guytrash' (see Glossary) was seen at Nooking Well, too, in the form of a black dog that was sometimes seen to disappear into a well.

WELL ON THE GREEN

Grid Ref SE1786 3771

Idle

This well is still in position though dry and the metal work has been removed. The remains of two taps are to be seen on the reverse. It consists of a stone well house with the date 1850 carved on the top slab. It is situated in a paved area between two ornamental trees.

BARKHILL WELL

Grid Ref SE1758 3752

Idle

On Highfield Road near Barkhill House this well was in the form of a trough. It served the house which was a very old settlement. The present house had had its name changed to Wellwood Bank in 1933. The well originated in the field near the house. 'Barkhill' gave its name from the practice of taking bark from oak trees for the Idle Tannery, an example of our own deforestation.

BURNWELLS

Grid Ref SE1730 3871

Idle

In a cul de sac off Windhill Old Road is the old settlement of Burnwells, which has some 18th century weavers houses and rows of cottages which was an old workhouse. Nearby was Jowett Farm, now demolished. The well, used for domestic purposes was positioned in the lane and consisted of a tall pump with a trough (see photo). The lane is surfaced with tarmac, otherwise it has not changed much, although the well has disappeared. A stream runs underground nearby. It ran openly through fields until housing was built around and on top of it in the 1970s and 1980s.

Burnwells last century.

In the 1853 *General Board of Health Report on Idle* six other wells are named but unfortunately the positions were not given. Therefore I have not been able to trace:

Causey or Causeway Well; Cordingley's Well; New York Well; Cam Well; Canker Well (said to be below the church).

There were other wells in Idle, every farm had one and even every allotment garden on Leeds Road had a trough which was fed by the network of channels.

BARREL WELL
Grid Ref SE1380 1040
Wibsey
Near Springwell Terrace and an old single storey group of cottages next to Beacon Road Medical Centre on Beacon Road is the Barrel Well,

Burnwells today (under manhole at bottom of photograph.)

set back in a stone walled alcove. Copious water was gushing out of the side of the solid stone-lined well, on my visit. A huge stone slab covers the well. The name comes from the time when a barrel could be filled without removing it from the cart.

CLAYTON
Until the late 19th century Clayton residents obtained their water from springs, mainly Low Well.

LOW WELL
Grid Ref SE1200 3210
Clayton
Two troughs at the south side of the present roundabout in the centre of Clayton were later moved to the middle of the road for watering animals. The roundabout was built around the wells. They are now dry and neglected.

HOLTS WELL

Grid Ref SE1165 3218

Clayton

Off Holts Lane, a bridle track north of the village, this well lies in a field overlooking Thornton. Two large slabs, one of them displaced, lie over a shallow well which contains some water. The name 'holte', meaning 'woodland', is mentioned in a 13th century document. There are no trees there now. There was another well at Town End or Teapot Spout (SE1190 3220), a medieval settlement.

Holts Well, Clayton.

WELL HEADS

Grid Ref SE0830 3326

Thornton

This well and area was called Wells Head in the 1890s. It is situated at Old Well Head Farm, Close Head Lane, and consists of three large stone troughs at the bottom of the farm garden (or orchard). They were full and overflowing on my visit in October 1992 when each trough was about 3 feet deep. The water was clear and flowing from one trough into another. In a dry season it slows to a trickle but does not dry up. It is being used for watering cattle.

Well Heads

There are wells in Scotland called 'well of the heads' (Bord and Bord 1985), the head being the skull of a saint or a substitute, from which a person wanting healing had to drink the well water. It is not impossible for this practice to have been performed here because stone heads have been found near to wells. On the other hand, the name Well Heads could be taken from the elevated position of the well.

JERUSALEM FARM WELLS
Grid Ref SE0850 3338
Thornton
This is the farm adjoining old Wells Heads. In *Pleasant Walks Around Bradford*, Speight says this farm gets its name from the Knights of St John of Jerusalem who owned the site and wrote that there were several wells there. Two of the wells have now been built over and the farm is now an abbatoir.

HARTLEY WELL SPRING
Grid Ref SE1150 3555
Well Lane, Bay of Biscay
Down a rough track between Bay of Biscay farm and the row of cottages is a long shallow stone basin with flowing water. I was told that the water is used locally.

Hartley Well Spring

CHELLOW WELLS

Grid Ref SE1224 3540

Chellow Grange

An old map shows a lane leading to two wells in a field which belonged to Chellow Grange Farm (part of a very old estate of the Bolling family of Bolling Hall). It was used for watering cattle but some people may have found the water beneficial for treating rheumatism. The area east of the wells became very marshy. In the 1920s a council housing estate was built around the march and over the site of the wells; this is Walden Drive. A football field was made over the marsh and the Council has had problems with drainage ever since.

MANYWELLS SPRING or SETH SPRING

Grid Ref SE0720 3570

Cullingworth

This is near Hewenden Reservoir, locally known as Seth Spring, but formerly called Manuels. 'The most interesting place to the casual visitor is the famous Manywells Spring which issues from the side of a steep hill at

Trooper, or Manywells Farm, a short distance from Hewenden Mill. This spring is one of the most extraordinary in the Kingdom, its volume increasingly poured forth having been computed at about half a million gallons a day. The quality of the water is well known - it is as cold as ice and as clear as crystal. This priceless spring has been found to issue from a fissure in the rock a short distance from the surface whence it literally belches forth into a massive basin and flows direct to Bradford seven miles away, the water being conducted in pipes to the store reservoirs at Chellow - almost the only source of supply. What an inexhaustible store this must have seemed to the Bradfordians of 1850. It was not secure until the Hewenden Reservoir was built.' (Cudworth 1876)

Today the spring is behind a locked door in the hillside, the water still rushing strongly under stone and concrete slabs to the reservoir. Hawthorn grows above it.

COLDWELL

Grid Ref SE0821 3620
Harecroft

This well is on a track called Nab Lane near the junction with Bents Lane. Cold Well Farm lies below the well and its waters are probably used there. The waters run off a field forming a muddy patch below which is the well, full of running water set against a dry stone wall. By itself this well would be most attractive, but next to it is a large square brick chamber with a concrete top. Water seeps through the brick. On the other side of the well is a modern bath with connecting pipe to the stone trough. In front of the bath are old gateposts leading into the field above. It is all a bit of a muddle but within the area there is a hawthorn and an elder. In the field at the opposite side of the track there is another modern bath and, lower, a fenced off area with a willow. There is also a large ash tree in the field.

COLDSPRING or MOORHEAD WELL

Grid Ref SE0636
Cullingworth

At Coldspring Mill there is a well which flows into Manywells Beck. When I arrived to search for it I found an attractive pergola with climbers and shrubs around it. I thought that I had found a tastefully restored wellhead, but when I enquired, I was told that it was the septic tank! The well is at the side of a wall. A quarter of a mile away, to the east, is Coldspring House. The course of the Roman road from Manchester to Ilkley runs along the entrance road.

TOWN WELLS

Grid Ref SE1184 3741

Cottingley

The village existed at the time of the Domesday Book. The water of the well still runs under stone slabs at its site in the south corner of Cottingley Mills building on Cottingley Old Road. An old photograph showing the water being collected in buckets is little different from today. On the opposite side of the road is Archroyd. a house whose entrance is a stone arch which used to be the entrance to the estate of Cottingley House, now a nursing home. At Cottingley Bar at the bottom of Cottingley Old Road, the turnpike toll booth was situated on the south side of the Bradford to Bingley Road. Immediately behind it was a private bath house (shown on a map of 1890) probably fed from the stream issuing from the well. The stream emerges at the north side of the main road and finds its way down to the river after feeding a fish pond.

Cottingley Wells from an old postcard

On the east side of the main road in the village was the Old Hall which existed from ancient times. Speight says he saw signs of an old 'entrenchment' and that the site may have been moated, the beck forming two sides of the boundary. In the 1890s, the Old Hall Well still stood beside the beck (SE1195 3099). The Jacobean Old Hall was considered to be a Templar house, as on the roof were a double-cross and stone lanterns, motifs of the Knights of St John of Jerusalem who took over many Templar possessions. The Old Hall was demolished in 1872 and there is now a block of flats on the site. The Old Hall Well site found, by dowsing, to be still flowing but hidden under rubble.

40

The present Sun Inn is situated above the old Sun Inn, which stood at the south side of the beck from the old hall. One of the buildings still forms part of the Old Sun Garage (SE1195 3705).

FLAPPIT SPRING
Grid Ref SE0765 3238
Flappit
Flappit is a hamlet where there are two springs, probably connected. Brick lined basins in the field have connecting pipes to a stone lined well in the first of a row of domed vaults, probably underneath a building at one time. Another spring lies to the south, utilised for cattle. There are 'Many Wells' here, even more than at the area called 'Manywells' further north neaer Cullingworth.

Baildon Moor

JOE'S WELL
Grid Ref SE1477 4088
Baildon Moor
This well was named after Joseph Batley of Baildon. It was also called Crag Well and is situated on Baildon Moor. Lucy Gill in *Baildon memories* wrote: 'It is said that the pure, never failing water of the well on the hillside above Low Hill [SE151409] was often drunk as a cure for whooping cough and also that it was used by the bar Committee of the Baildon Working Mens Club from its openig in 1892 to "break down the rum and gin which they bought in bulk". The water was considered to "impart to the spirit a flavour and character unsurpassed by any sold in the district".'

Low Hill, Sconce (SE148412) and Moorside (see Moorside wells) were all small hamlets where miners lived last century. Most of the houses have been demolished because of supposed unsanitary conditions.

It was when Baildon village wells became polluted that a man who called himself 'Dinnas' (Joseph Halliday) toured the village by horse and cart selling the water for ½d a pail full (or 'kit' as it was known).

This well is now difficult to find, especially when the bracken is high. It consists of a square flagged chamber completely enclosed, with an exit pipe at the top. No water was coming out of the pipe at the time of my visit in August 1992 because the drought had lowered the water level. A boggy stream seeping from the base was the only water I could see.

ACRE WELL

Grid Ref SE1480 4060

Baildon

This well was by Acre Cottage on Baildon Moor, near the Bronze Age tumulus Acre Howe and Acre Howe Cross. As with Joe's Well, its waters were also transported to Baildon Village by 'Dinnas'. In the 1850s the water was diverted into newly-built reservoirs to increase the water supply to the village. The cottage was demolished and all that is left now is a boggy hollow by the golf course. The reservoirs are not now in use.

CRUTCH WELL

Grid Ref SE1470 3870

Baildon Green

This was a natural spring which was widened out in order to lessen flooding onto the nearby road to Baildon but it is still an attractive spot. Water cress used to grow in it, as it does in the lower course of the issuing stream. Its name and purpose is now practically lost amongst the locals but the name implies that it was a healing well where people threw away their crutches after being healed, as was a tradition at other such wells. The water flows under the road and used to cool the drinks in the cellar of the Cricketers Arms but now it flows outside the building. The pub was built this century on the site of a quarry. The well has a tradition (repeated in local history books) of never running dry, a characteristic of a holy or healing well.

Above it on Baildon Bank are Robin Hood's House and Cloven Stones, a site of fairies and goblins. Also near the well was the Early or Hurley Stone, near which centred pranks committed by young men around Whit Saturday. The origin of the prank (performed yearly) is unknown, as is the stone. An Arley Stone or Early Stone existed as a boundary stone on the Roman road, Harden Moor. There used to be another spring on the bank called Sheep Dyke which must have dried up. There is a deep draw well on the mill premises in this hamlet.

BINNSWELL

Grid Ref SE154397

Baildon

At the top of Binnswell Fold was a shallow well, although a child was drowned there in 1801. He was Joseph, the son of Thomas Mawson, a wool worker. A row of cottages near the well has been demolished and the area has

Crutch Well.

been made into a car park for Baildon Methodist Church and the Link. Cellars in the lower part of the fold are flooded from time to time which suggests the well or the source of its water is still there.

Before gaslight came to Westgate the well was haunted by the Guytrash Padfoot and the White Woman.

LOIN SPAHT

Grid Ref SE1529 3960

Tentercroft

This well was a healing well for those with fertility problems, rather an unusual designation for this region. The well is seen on an old photograph in *Pictures of Old Baildon* (Entwistle 1985). It is

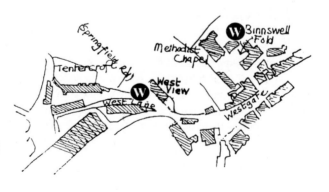

Loin Spaht and Binnswell, Baildon 1891.

West View, Westgate, Baildon. In the hole in the wall is Loin Spaht or Loyn Spout Well. Photo taken before 1935 when road widened.

shown as a square hole at the bottom of a wall in a hollow in front of cottages at the corner of Springfield Road and West Lane. In 1935 the area was filled in and part of Tentercroft hamlet demolished in order to widen West Lane at that point.

FAR WELL

Grid Ref SE1528 3922

Baildon

At the bottom of the cliff on Green Road, Lane End, next to a garden wall, this well site still exists, hidden by undergrowth. It was said to be medicinal. There are signs of a stream bed above it. The well is a sunken trough a few feet deep covered with a metal grate. Whether there is water in it now is doubtful. It used to supply Sandals Pond (SE1520 3910). This pond may have been formed after sand extraction.

Another version of Sandal Pond's origin is given in *Round About Bradford* by Cudworth. He says, 'It was made at the instance of Major

Meyers of Baildon Hall. Having a troop of government cavalry billeted at the Hall, he employed men and horses in making this pond (to supply fish) and the road [Green Road] being conveyed to an eminence from whence the soldiers might be seen reviewing. It is still called Major Gate.' In the 1890s, skating was popular on the pond. It was filled in in the 1960s, after becoming silted up because of a diminishing of the water supply, and is now a park.

NEAR WELL or FRANKS WELL
Grid Ref SE1525 3920
Baildon
Situated south of Lane End Farm. Ingham Greenwood, the farmer, would let people use his well *if* he was in a good mood. Modern housing and a medical centre now occupy the site which is next to Sandals First School.

EAGLANDS WELL
Grid Ref SE1575 3970
Baildon
At the eastern end of Hall Cliffe, adjoining Batley House, this well was in the form of a trough. Although it has disappeared, water oozes up from the road. The position of the well was significant as it was on an old track from Bingley to Otley which kept to the high ground. It is also situated at a five-lanes-end where major tracks meet, one of which was Holden Lane which connects it to Halliwell Banks Well.

At Batley House there is an 80 feet deep draw well, now filled and situated underneath the conservatory.

At the foot of Cliffe Lane was 'a splendid spring'. People living in Baildon and working in Shipley often brought the water home. Wellfield is a local place-name and a Moravian chapel stood near the well. Cliffe Lane is probably on the site of an ancient trackway leading to the moor.

HELLIWELL BANKS WELL
Grid Ref SE1610 3962
Baildon
The name confirms there was a holy well here, in Helliwell Banks Wood, alternatively called Halliway. It was first mentioned in 1490 in the Baildon Court Rolls. It is situated above the Kirkfields and had a path leading to it. By tradition it was haunted by a spectral hound with

large glowing red eyes. Holden Lane, one of the early tracks to Baildon, passed near to the well. The boggard was seen here and Slaughter Lane, the present Kirkfields Lane. In the 19th century the well waters were piped off in various directions to large residences and to public troughs on Holden Lane and Kirklands Lane. It is now capped by the water authority. Around it lies a jumble of stones, perhaps a remnant of a more orderly enclosure. A pipe connects it to the remains of another two wells on the western side of the wood. Housing is being built in Kirkfields at present.

BOBBLING WELL

Grid Ref SE1550 3972

Baildon

There is a plaque above the well, put there by Baildon Urban District Council in 1933, which is near the Malt Shovel inn. The pipe and the basin are now firmly cemented up and flagged over.

The stream which fed the well at one time came freely down Northgate but was gradually covered over. The first trough to be constructed was by the Pinfold at a position where the sweetshop hut is now. It was called Old Ike Well. Later it was moved across the road and stood where the Copper Beech Club is. Then, after the cottage next to the Malt Shovel was demolished, it was erected in its present position and renamed Bobbling Well.

The water was said to be slightly chalybeate, containing iron of medicinal value and was liked by animals (although one source says that animals did not like it). It provided water for the tan pit which was next to the Malt Shovel.

WELLS AT MOORSIDE

Grid ref SE156404

Baildon Moor

There are three natural springs within yards of each other along the track here. Moorside Equestrian Centre is the only house left now in this former hamlet. The well at the eastern side has a carved stone spout with a natural basin below while rough stone walls shore up the banking around it. It is the more attractive of the springs and may have been the one used for drinking water. The other two were used for all other purposes according to Lucy Gill's *Baildon memories*. Modern baths are now used as receptacles at the other wells.

MITTON SPRING

Grid Ref SE1327 3961

Baildon Moor

The Rev Thomas Mitton who owned the spring sold the water for ½d for three gallons and transported it by a water cart to sell to Baildon people, who continued to buy the water after a piped supply was laid on because it was cheaper. The reverend said it cost him as much as 6d in dry weather. Today the spring is an uninviting puddle just above the wall of the wood of the same name. Signs of iron deposits lie on the surface of the mud.

ST IVES WELL

Grid Ref SE0960 3829

Harden Grange, Harden

St Ives, a Persian Bishop appeared in a dream to an English peasant in 1001AD to verify that the body which had recently been found, with others, was his. The body was transferred to Ramsey Abbey where, through a spring of water issuing near to it, miracles of healing took place.

Was the old St Ives (now Harden Grange) built around a healing spring? A well is said to be covered up in the cellar. The present St Ives House has within its grounds a spring which still provides a water supply and flows into a small reservoir at SE0924 3909.

ST ANTONY'S WELL

Grid Ref 0851 3850

Harden

This well is on Antony Lane, which is a narrow track. This track was also called Old Ike Hill, after an evil spirit or the devil (see Old Ike Well, Baildon). A plaque marks the well site, put there by the Harden Village Society, otherwise it could be missed as a small stone channel in the wall is all that can be seen. In very wet weather the water runs but it is otherwise dry. There used to be a trough beneath but it was stolen.

St Antony of Egypt (251-356AD) was a protector of animals. He founded a hospital and his hospitallers rode about ringing little bells. Afterwards the bells were hung around the necks of animals, especially pigs, to protect them from disease. This tradition seems to have been translated into the baking of 'Parkin Pigs' (see Glossary) locally in Bingley. It is suggested that the Norse god Frey was the pre-Christian deity which St Antony supplanted because Frey was associated with the boar that was sacrificed to him at Yule. Perhaps in Christian times Frey became Old Ike, if the tradition with this well goes back that far. but the custom could be overlapped by pagan symbolism too. There was another St Antony's well at North0wram (see page 53).

WHITE WELL
Grid Ref SE0890 3835
Harden

This well is in the grounds of Harden Memorial Hall, completely hidden by a sycamore seedling, but over it grows a large ash tree. The well consists of an iron bath, rounded at one end. A trickle of water comes out of a modern pipe into the beck next to the well. The overflow flows into another beck which flows a short way then disappears under playing fields.

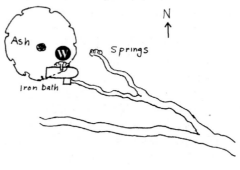

White Well, Harden

ABBEY WELL
Grid Ref SE0972 3638
Norr

The hamlet of Norr near Wilsden is of a very old foundation, Kirkstall Abbey owned it up to the Dissolution. Some buildings are 17th century; stone heads are built in to a porch wall and there are some very old wells.

Abbey Well was situated at the end of a row of cottages which used to be known as Black Abbey, now called Norr. Timbers in the roof came from a ship from Hull.

The well was open until the 1950s but is now filled in although the water still runs beneath a lawn. Speight described it in the 1890s as 'ever full' and it may have been used as a cure for gravel. There was an old elder tree next to it until recently and a smaller one still grows over the wall which suggests it was planted to be a protective tree for the well. A farmer, Hartley Riddiough, fell into the well as a boy when he lived in the cottage in about 1910.

48

CLAREMONT FARM WELL

Grid Ref SE0970 3645

Norr

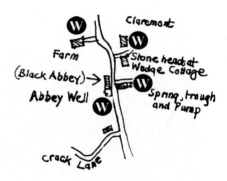

Wells at Norr.

Known as T'Abba Farm, the buildings were converted into cottages in 1820 but is now one house. The well still runs by an outbuilding behind the house.

There are two or three other wells in Norr, one of which at Norr Farm has the remains of an old pump and a huge stone trough by the public footpath to Norr Hill.

CATSTONE WELL

Grid Ref SE0670 3782

Harden Moor

This well is situated to the south of the ancient earthwork of Catstone Ring and near to where monastic lead mining and smelting were carried out. It lies about 200 yards east of the Roman road from Manchester to Ilkley. A considerable amount of water flows from the well at a dip in the field next to the moor. The present receptacles for the water consist of a metal trough and a rusty drum inside a rough brick chamber. No doubt the cattle who drink the water do not care about the lack of aesthetic qualities. There are no trees in the vicinity.

DUCKING WELL

Grid Ref SE0320 3677

Haworth

There was a ducking pond, where unruly women were 'ducked', at the Coldshaw (south) end of Haworth for hundreds of years; its present position being at the junction of Sun Street and Cold Street which was originally the village green. Later it was reduced to a well at the side of the road, shown on the 1893 map, although a photograph shows it in a central 'island'. This would make the Haworth Council's decision to move it to the side of the road understandable, because it was obstructing traffic. In 1932, after not having water in it for about 20 years, it was moved again to the brand new park. Due to vandalism and rubbish at the site, the well, in the form of a trough, was

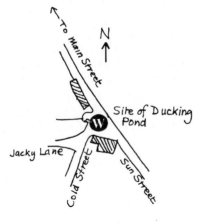

The site of the Ducking Well in 1993

broken up about 1983. It could easily have been erected in the central 'island' where now there is a seat and a cherry tree.

TRUE WELL
Grid Ref SE0282 4016
Newsholme near Laycock

This well is at True Well Hole (now Hall) Farm. The nature of the name strongly implies that it was a prechristian well of great power from which the Christian priests tried to turn their flock to the 'approved' Jennett's Well at Black Hill above Keighley. On the 1852 OS map a path runs from the well to Brown Hill to the west. The well lies above Newsholme Beck which runs through a gorge at this point.

The present farmhouse is mainly 16th century but may have been built on an older site. The well, in a field a few yards above the house, is still there with some water, partially covered by slabs. The stump of a large ash tree lies to the north and there are a few other ash trees to the south and in a small woodland. The water once flowed to a trough in the yard which has an attractively carved lintel. The water was then piped to another trough near the barn door. They are now filled with earth and plants.

The family of Shackleton, the Arctic explorer, lived in the house and the area for many generations. The farm is now a riding stables.

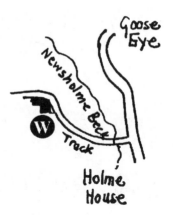

True Well, Laycock.

True Well, Laycock.

Peggy Well, Riddlesden showing sheep dip trough.

PEGGY WELL

Grid Ref SE0655 4413

Riddlesden

Near the moor, this well is off a footpath which leads through a field from Holden Gate. The natural spring issues from very large boulders. Three ash trees grow around the site. Below the well the water is directed into an old stone lined sheep dipping trough. Holden Gate is a very old farmstead which used to obtain its water supply from the well. The well's name may be derived from the water spirit 'Peg' who gave her name to other wells. The Robin Hood Stone lies nearby on the moor.

JENNET'S WELL

Grid Ref SE0465 4182

Keighley

At Blackhills high above Keighley on the western side is this little well. It is situated on Shann Lane by an old attractive cottage clad with Virginia creeper. A stone trough lies half way under a wall and the water flows from behind, overflowing into a grate at the side of the road. The water supplied the whole of Keighley last century. In pre-Reformation times priests

Jennet's Well, Blackhills, Keighley.

encouraged people to visit this well instead of another one called True Well because the people paid too much attention to the latter because its pagan influence was too strong.

ALDERS WELL
Grid Ref SE16714168
Hawksworth
This well is in the middle of an overgrown wood next to the main road and the old kitchen garden of Hawksworth Hall. An insignificant pipe and earth channel is all that can be seen. It was not marked on a map of 1811.

BIRKIN WELL
Grid Ref SE1765 4143
Hawksworth
This well, originally called Birkhill (from birch trees), was described in the 16th century by Alistair Laurence as being in a series of fields called Hall Croft, belonging to Hawksworth Hall. It may have existed in the 14th century when the old Hall was known to exist. The area became parkland with deer in the 17th century but it is now a golf course. The well, in the form of a trough

53

with a good flow of water, is at the bottom of a slope a few yards from the public footpath across the course. There was a public way across the field called 'Willow Lane', along which was Tofts Well. This has now disappeared.

SUNNYBANK WELL
Grid Ref SE1623 4068
Baildon
Southwards in Tong Park, in the woods is this natural spring.

GUISELEY WELLS
Grid Ref SE1930 4215
Guiseley
Guiseley owes its existence to the Guiseley Wells which were the main water supply of the village for hundreds of years. In Rigg's *Round About Aireborough* someone was quoted as saying in 1795 'There was not a single pump or well in Guiseley except the town wells'.

More recent references from Rigg include: 'The Guiseley wells were bubbling up with beautiful water under the great trees which overshadowed

Guiseley Wells.

them' (Rector's letter of 1930). 'Many scholars late because of fetching water from the wells due to drought' (log book of Church School). 'Old Folks fetched jugs of pure water for Sunday lunch. . . . In the 1920s boreholes were dug and altered the water flow. . . . The troughs must have been built to deepen the water so buckets could more easily be filled.' (Rigg *Round About Aireborough*).

The wells are arranged in a long row of eight troughs at the base of a dry stone wall with part of another trough half hidden at one end. Referring to the number nine which is a significant number in folklore, I am reminded of this tale: 'If a maiden visited the Nine Wells at Hall Royd and washed her handkerchief in each one she would see who was to be her husband - so it was said' (passed on by Rayner in *The History of Pudsey*). I do not know which wells the tale referred to.

At the wells is now a plaque which reads: 'Guiseley Wells round which this township grew. This plaque was presented by Aireborough and Horsforth Musem Society 1972'.

At one time there were railings round the wells, but now, although there is plenty of flowing water, none of the troughs are deep. There has been some restoration and the level of the road raised so there are now two steps down to the wells. The area in front of the troughs where the water overflows was the hard standing for the washing of carts.

ST ANTHONY'S WELL

Grid Ref SE111 264

Haugh Top, Northowram

St Antony of Egypt (251 - 356) gave his name to many wells which were particularly connected with the healing of animals. This well was mentioned in a deed of 1535. A house called 'Springhead Lodge', built in 1749 was formerly called Anthony Well according to Heggingbotham. The well was indicated at the gable end of Springhead Lodge on the first edition OS map. There is no sign of the well today.

(See St Antony Well, Harden [page 47] and Parkin Pigs in Glossary).

TOMBLING WELL

Grid Ref SE2056 3788

Calverley Wood

This well is reached from Wood Lane which runs southwards from the main road. The lane which led to old quarries in the wood is at first lined by an old hedge of cherry, plum and other fruit and nut trees bordering allotments. At a lodge there are two choices of route to the well which is just past a walled embankment on the low road towards the canal. The spring emerges from beneath a large holly tree and beside it is another large holly. It may be that the hollies were planted over the well in their role as a holy, protective tree. Today the site is overgrown and can easily be missed. Large stones suggest previous enclosing of the well. The water was flowing in a slow trickle in August 1993.

There was a tradition, reported by Speight, that it never ran dry. Cup and ring stones were dug up nearby.

TOWN WELLS

Grid Ref SE2090 3691
Calverley

These wells were described as being 'on the green in the centre of the village', so there is some doubt whether this is the original site but the water is there. Four shallow troughs, not running much when visited in summer 1992, are in a very attractive sunken public garden with limestone rocks, stone chipping paths, conifers, rock plants and seats. They are situated on the north-east side of the village immediately north of the main road in half an acre of garden. Mature sycamore and beech line the

Town Wells, Calverley.

road side. The wells are very shallow but may have been made so for safety reasons.

FAREWELL

Grid Ref SE2136 3655
Calverley
This healing well gave its name to Farewell Ings and Farewell Closes by 1665. On modern maps it is marked as chalybeate but is now covered over by the water board.

LADY WELL

Grid Ref SE1684 4323
Menston
This well still exists in a debased form, situated in a field called Lady Well Close, near a public footpath off Bingley Road. It consists of a long concrete trough 12 ft x 2 ft fed by a pipe above a low stone wall. At one time it was in a well house with steps leading down to it. Fletcher (*The Story of Menston* 1953) says 'it was like a Roman Bath'. The site is near a constituency boundary and High Royds Hall, an old farm, from which the nearby High Roads Hospital takes its name. It is also not very far (half-a-mile) from a 12th century boundary and possibly ancient trackway

Lady's Well, Menston.

which ran from White Cross along Tranmire Beck to York Gate on Ilkley Moor. Until last century sword dancers rehearsed and performed in front of the Well House.1665.

WEST WOOD WELL

Grid Ref SE1978 3740

Calverley

The wood in which the well is found was part of the Calverley family estate, but more recently has passed into different ownership.

In 1605 Walter Calverley murdered two of his sons but was caught and condemned. According to Cudworth's *Roundabout Bradford Vol II*, it was said that he would continue to haunt the scene of the murder while 'holly grew green in Calverley Wood'. There were also reports that he 'galloped about through his extensive wood at dead of night on a headless horse, with agonising cries. His favourite 'haunt' was a cave under the Hanging Stone. This area has been quarried and the cave destroyed and so the ghost is laid.

There was an ancient footpath through the wood, near to the cave and the well, which was altered in the 1850s when there was a plan to 'develop' the wood and lay out extensive roads. Compensation was offered to the villagers by conveying water to three places in the village. In the event, only a small part of the wood was developed and there was just one building around the well. It is a most interesting well which has running water. It is almost totally enclosed within a flat-topped stone chamber built around natural rocks. One can sit inside on a protruding shelf. There is a door and the remains of a chain which was probably attached to a drinking cup. The well is heavily overhung

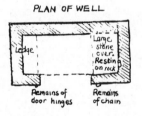

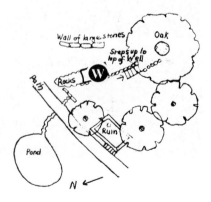

West Wood Well, Calverley.

with ivy and rhododendron while oak is the prominent tree. Steps nearby lead to an area at the top of the well bounded by a huge boulder wall. The water runs to a stone lined pond at the other side of the track. Could this have been a small spa? (See Cudworth *Round About Bradford).*

TONG WELL

Grid Ref SE2221 3065

Tong

A stream runs under the main road at the junction of Keeper Lane and shows itself briefly within a walled area. Originally the water was directed to a stone pillar where it flowed out of a lion's mouth into a trough below. The gaping mouth now looks odd without its stream of water. Nearby is a pinfold preserved and indicated by a plaque commemorating it as a European Heritage site. Surely the well and its lion are worth of similar recognition?

SMALE WELL

Grid Ref SE2121 3280

Pudsey

This well was described by historians as 'being in a stark precipice, toilsome of ascent' where only cattle drank. Such was its position that there was 'no idol there because pilgrims could not be made to pay'. The word

Tong Well with lion spout.

'smale' was probably from the Icelandic word, *smali*, meaning 'small cattle', but also 'sheep' and 'goats'. In that area 'all the fence divisions are stone walls and the Royding so effectual' that there were no trees from which to replace the hedges. The woods had been clearly assarted and, at the time W. Wheater was writing between 1860 and 1890 (cited in Rayner), 'the same had recently been done across Tyersal Beck'.

In 1847 Smalewell was shown on the map to be on the side of Tyersal Lane, part way down the hill. Before World War I, Fartown Football Club used to take the ball down to the well to wash it.

The well has been lost now, but a little further down the lane there is an old trough embedded in a wall at the corner of Smalewell Gardens which the same water may have run into.

JUMBLES WELL
Grid Ref SE21343271
Pudsey

This well, known in 1799, was a holy well according to Rayner. According to his *History of Pudsey,* an ancient path (shown on the 1847 OS map) from Chapel Town to Windmill Lane was 'a span away from the well'. 'The well was of special adoration to our ancestors both Norse and Angle. On the reintroduction of Christianity after the deluge of Danish Paganism, the priests were exhorted to wean the flock away from the old objects of praise'. More recently locals 'frequented the well on Sundays'. In 1887 it still remained in a degraded state, on a hill west of the green at Over Pudsey.

Now the well has been destroyed as road widening and building have taken place within living memory. It was by the road near the 'Fox and Grapes'.

GRIFF WELL

Grid Ref SE1550 2620

Wyke

This well is probably now in the grounds of a modern house because on or near its position there is a very mature ash tree. Originally in the grounds of Griff House near Griff Head where there was a pinfold. Modern street names nearby retain the word 'Griff'.

ING WELL and WHEATCROFT WELL

Grid Ref SE1555 2610 and SE1558 1215

Wyke

By the side of the main Whitehall Road are attractive fields with mature hedges, where horses and ponies graze. The wells rise at the corners of the fields but they cannot be seen from the road and there is no access. One of the streams is marked on recent OS maps.

VILLAGE WELL

Grid Ref SE1978 2910

East Bierley

The village of East Bierley has kept its village green intact. The well, once a

East Bierley village well. The well is immediately behind the tree which has been pruned. The stump cross and pond lie in front of Cross House.

draw well 30ft deep, was restored in 1978 when a small pump was attached to the wall next to the well. It has since lost the pump, most of it has been filled in and a grid near the top inserted. It is situated on a connecting piece of land between two parts of the green. The green has an attractive large duck pond, a stump cross and, adjoining it, Cross House (dated 1662). The green also has two old mark stones, one having signs of carving, and the village stocks. A pinfold stood nearby and, a little to the east, Moor House is dated 1632.

HEALY WELL OAK

Grid Ref SE2322 2879
Drighlington
In the south-east corner between two arable fields is a spring. It issues from a large pipe and was flowing strongly on my visit early 1992. The stream flows towards the east in a cutting. The area is very overgrown with brambles and tall weeds even in winter. There are no trees at the point of entry but there are hawthorn hedges in the area. A little further along the stream is a small 'forest' of elders. Unfortunately rubbish has been allowed to accumulate here. The site is very near the Roman road and the medieval settlement of Adwalton. 'Healy' is a corruption of holy. The oak which grew here has long since gone.

LADY WELL

Grid Ref SE1790 2350
Hartshead
The well is situated along Lady Well Lane, a track leading to Hartshead church, a quarter of a mile from Walton Cross. It is marked by a single hawthorn and is in the form of a trough sunk into the ground with a stone dividing the two halves, one on the road side and one on the field side. The trough on the field side was full of water when visited though static. The stream which fed it now runs beside it. On the road side it is filled with rubble.

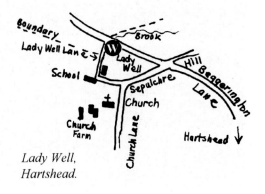

Lady Well, Hartshead.

*Lady Well,
Hartshead.*

St Peter's church, Hartshead, is of ancient foundation, dating back to 500AD and in the graveyard on the south side are the remains of the old yew tree, said to exist before the church was built. By tradition, Robin Hood made his bow from this tree and he is buried in the grounds of Kirklees Hall just over the hill. The stream running from the well trickles down towards Hightown. In some places there are traditions of processions from churches to the local Holy well.

FAIRY WELL
Grid Ref SE1981 2308
Roberttown

This well is situated in fields off the main road near Pogg Myers. Under a bank with a tall hedge on top and half-covered with a large stone slab, the well is lined with brick and stone and quite deep, but is filled with soil and silt. Water rises from the field below. There is a large elder above the well, which is within a hawthorn hedge. It seems to be significant because elder is a tree associated with wells and a protection against witches and fairies. Birds

63

nests are in evidence above and male fern grows in the well. A tall wire fence cuts off the well from the field.

DRUB SPA
Grid Ref SE1937 2680
Drub
This little spa was at Mazebrook near Drub, Cleckheaton. Mazebrook is an old farmstead in an elevated position near to a brook which runs through a small, tree-lined valley. Speight, in *Pleasant Walks Around Bradford*, says that people came from long distances for treatment of rheumatism. It was open daily except Thursdays and Sundays.

Halifax area

HOLY WELL or LISTERS WELL
Grid Ref SE1320 2632
Priestley Green
Two stone troughs sunk into the pavement lie under large slabs of stone. They collect the water which flows into a smaller open trough. It is directed under the gate of Priors Mead and its garden to a pond at Holroyd House and thence to Coley Beck. The lady who lives in one of the Sisters houses told me in 1992 that the well had a better flow in the past and that fresh water shrimps used to live in the well.

The well lies in front of the Sisters House, an old 17th century row of cottages. By tradition the sisters who resided there each built a chapel - Coley Chapel and Lightcliffe Chapel, each the same distance from their house in opposite directions. The origins of the cottages go back to the 13th century. Can we assume that the well was there before the house was built? The well seems to have been demoted from 'holy' to 'Lister', probably reflecting the declining interest in the specialness of holy wells. In its day, it was said to 'possess magic cures for all who drank its crystal waters and pilgrimages were made to it - it is a grand type of a country well not often met with in these modern days' (Cudworth *From Hipperholme to Tong* 1904). The flow of water is now not as great as it was 30 years ago because of drainage work in the watershed and because of the lowering water table.

Listers Well, Priestley Green.

HELLIWELL SYKE WELL
Grid Ref SE1326 1206
Priestley Green

This gives it name to Helliwell Syke Lane, Helliwell Sike (the stream which issues from the well), Helliwell Syke Farm (now demolished) and the local surname Helliwell. The well consists of four stone troughs together in a little lay-by by the side of Helliwell Syke Lane. A stone spout directs the water into one of the central troughs, all of which were full on inspection, the two outermost having a layer of duckweed on the surface. On the other side of the wall in a field is a plastic trough for cattle. Two large ash trees grow in the field behind the well. The water flows under the road and the stream leads into Coley Beck.

ST JOHN'S WELL
Grid Ref SE1286 2710
Coley Hall

Tradition tells us that there was a Priory or Hospital of the Knights Templars or the Knights of St John on the site of the present Coley Hall. The earliest reference to the hall's existence is in 1371. 'In the field at the high side of the hall was [and is] St John's well, supposed to have been used for

65

Halliwell Syke Well.

certain complaints'
(Parker *From Hipper-
holme to Tonge*).

The spring is marked
on present-day maps. The
main well is a circular
stone shaft about 5 ft
deep, covered over with
large stone slabs. Water
still flows underground.
All the wells around
Coley and Priestley Green
were blessed by Roman
Catholic priests and were
supposed to possess heal-
ing powers *if* the priests
anointed the waters before
the people came to drink.

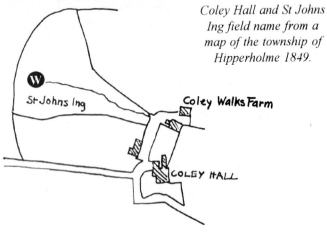

*Coley Hall and St Johns
Ing field name from a
map of the township of
Hipperholme 1849.*

St Johns Ing

Coley Walks Farm

COLEY HALL

Halifax

ST JOHN THE BAPTIST'S WELL
or JONAS WELL

Grid Ref SE 0973 2530
Halifax

'In the deep valley where the church now stands was a Hermitage dedicated to St John the Baptist' - which attracted pilgrims who travelled on tracks from four directions called 'Hollyways' to the Hermitage (Allen, *History of the County of York*, 1831 citing Camden's *Brittania*). The well of St John the Baptist may have been at that spot, about 200 yards north of St John the Baptist's church. So important was the St John connection, legendary or not, that the motif of the head of the saint found its way to the coat of arms of Halifax.

The well was famous for its powers of healing so can definitely be classed as a holy well. Later it became known as Jonas Well. In the last century it was marked on OS maps and was seen to be in the grounds of Multure Hall. It was also used as a water supply for Halifax in the 19th century, filling troughs and being directed to another trough at the side of Jonas Well Lane. The well as it appeared then was described by Armitage (*Halifax Antiquary* 1969) as 'an open basin 6 ft x 3 ft 6 ins and 4 ft deep'. It was flagged over and covered with earth, possibly to protect it. The site is now just over the wall on Multure Hall Road next to the Woolmerchants Hotel. It is a derelict site awaiting 'development'. How about a plaque to mark its position?

I speculate that one of the Hollyways could have run from Popplewell above Warley, down Gibbet Street, through Crown Street, Gaol Lane and Well Lane, to the well. This is because near to Popplewell a medieval track and the Roman road from Manchester to Ilkley meet (Grid Ref SE0542 2519).

HOLY WELL

Grid Ref SE1000 2540
Halifax

On Old Bank 270 yards from the parish church at Folly Steps was another holy well. The Old Bank was the main road to Wakefield in medieval times, then called the Magna Via. It was a holloway, a narrow packhorse route leading up the steep bank of Beacon Hill which led eventually to

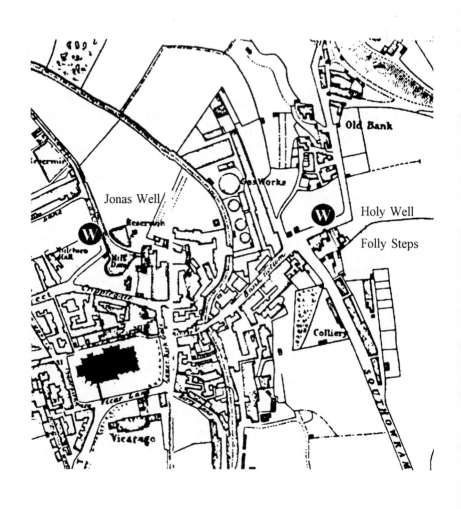

Jonas Well

Old Bank

Holy Well

Folly Steps

Map of Halifax 1842 with positions of Jonas Well,
Holy Well and Folly Steps shown.

68

Wakefield. The track still exists and is marked by a plaque. There were a group of cottages nearby, mentioned in the 18th century as Holy Well, but later the name was changed to Folly Steps. The cottages were demolished in the 1950s. The well, in a derelict state, could be seen under a broken cover when visited in 1992.

GREAT HORTON

Suburbia has encroached much here since 1847 when the first OS map was produced. Many wells are clearly shown but not any of them named. James Parker in his *Great Horton in Bye-gone days* (1900) reproduces a list of *Old Place names in Great Horton, mostly obsolete.* They include the following wells (with my grid references where identifiable):

'Ca' Wells old wells, now done away with, top of Brow Hill

Union Well Southfield Lane, back of Wheatsheaf

*Spring Head Well Aycliffe Hill [SE1444 3095]

Jacky Well Pickles Lane, named after Jacky Dracup [SE1367 3085]

Beldon Hill Well Beldon Hill [SE1378 3075]

Old Road Well (four possibilities)

Jer Loine Well Jer Loine [SE1301 3081]

Hollingwood Lane Well [SE1300 3106]

Trough Field Well

Sugar Well near the Old Corn Mill, Beckside

Town End Well near Toby Lane

*On a modern map the well at Haycliffe Hill is the only one marked. A natural spring, it rises behind the old Methodist Chapel (now a house) but the flow is a mere trickle. It used to supply Bradford with water at the same time as the Manywells Spring was brought into use.

Queensbury

Barratt, in *A History of Queensbury* (1963) gave a 'complete' list of the wells, reproduced below. He writes that in 1867 there was a scare about a possible fever epidemic caused by impure drinking water, but, after testing the wells, they were found to be wholesome.

Shibden Head Well	private
Ambler Thorn Well	private
Roper Lane Well	public
Moor Close Lane Bottom Well	public

Swamp Well	public
Walker Lane, Swamp, Well	public
Emsley's Pump, Swamp	private
Sour Heads Well,	
(back of Old Queens Head)	public
Granby Pump	private
Boundary Place Pump	private
Bairstow's Pump, Moor End	private
The Fountain, Albert Square	private
Hungerhill Pump	private
Booth's Pump, Sandbeds	private
New House Farm Well	private
Scarlet Height Pump	private
Brickfield Pump	private
Sharket Head Well	private
Knowles Pump	private
Hill Top Well	public
Spring Head Well	private
Broomfield Well	private
Patchett's Pump, Mountain	private
Catherine Slack Well	public

There are many other wells marked on the 1847 OS map, Queensbury being quite 'well endowed', but most of them will now be lost or capped.

The lost hamlet of Cockham (or Cockin)

Grid Ref SE1031

Clayton Parish

This hamlet was mentioned in old deeds from the 14th to the 18th centuries, but after that the name disappeared from all references to the area. It was situated in the parish of Clayton. In the reign of Queen Ann, Clayton was divided into three areas, Town (the village), Height (Clayton Heights) and Cockham. Cockham was probably centred on Hole Bottom, the site of the latter Queensbury Station. It was probably a scattered community mostly living in wooden houses which have rotted without trace, but within the hamlet there were stone built houses and farms which still exist.

The relevance to this work is that there were four old wells:- Hurstwells, Merwell, Dakwell and Turnwell. There are many wells indicated in 19th

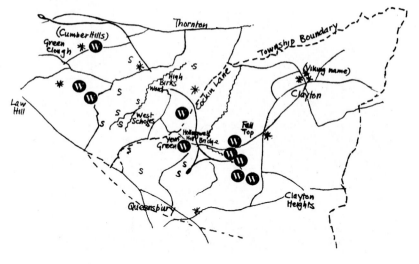

The lost hamlet of Cockham
*S - spring   * - medieval site*

century maps but the sites of the above wells are not known. However, there are clues. There is a Hollingwell Hill near the Queensbury 'Triangle' (old station) where there is a row of cottages with a well marked in the field behind on the first edition OS map. This could indicate another lost holy well.

Dakwell was a watercourse, the probable stream being Hole Bottom Beck which is bridged by Brow Lane.

Westscholes is an old hall dating from 1694 probably replacing an earlier building. Speight said that around it were several old wells, one of which in the form of two troughs on a track opposite the hall. At Fall Top on Brook Lane was a medieval settlement. Here there are three wells still intact with drinkable water, connected to each other.

There are several other wells. The western boundary of Clayton Township lies along Cockin Lane and Lane Side to Mountain, yet there are four medieval houses (or sites) over the boundary: Westscholes, Green Clough, Lower Sandal and Upper Headley Hall all with associated wells. The population of Cockham in the 16th century was large, consisting of about 250 people (Faull and Moorhouse). In the 18th century changing fortunes must have obliged many of them to migrate to the neighbouring towns and villages

Westscholes, Cockham.

leaving a depleted community of farms which were affected at the beginning of the 19th century by enclosures and in the middle of that century by the railway.

Ilkley

Ilkley is famous for its major Roman fort 'Olicana' which had important Roman roads leading to and from it in four cardinal directions. The parish church was later built on the site and forms the centre of the present town. The Romans built a bath in or near their fort and would have obtained their water from one of the two streams which ran along two sides of the fort. One of the water sources was the brook which still runs off the moor and ran openly down Brook Street until the mid-19th century. Roman coins were found at the bottom of Wells Road by the brook which suggests it may have been a meeting point and a place where votive offerings were made to the Goddess 'Verbeia' although it was the river Wharfe itself which was the Goddess.

In the 18th century a large 'bath' was placed in the town centre to collect the waters of the brook and held 1150 gallons which filled in 13 minutes. In 1874 a fountain was erected at the top of Brook Street for passers-by to drink

72

the water. The chalybeate spring at the top of Hebers Ghyll was discovered in 1863 and the Canker Well lay in the gardens of the Hydropathic Establishment. In the later 19th century the Council bought much of the moorland adjoining the town from the squire, William Middleton, and today the water authorities make extensive use of the water supply from the moor.

Mill Ghyll, where once there were two cornmills, was given to the town in 1852 by Squire Middleton, and the waters still gush strongly before disappearing underground just before the reinstated 'fountain' which is now without its water and sculptured horses at the base but contains bedding plants. The water of the brook still rushes down Brook Street, but underground. In Mill Ghyll are some beautiful trees. Rooks nest in the sycamores nearest the fountain. This area was the site of the thatched cottage which became Lister's refreshment room in the 1850s; a meeting place where money was handled as the Romans did in that same spot nearly 2,000 years before.

STOR HILL WELL

Grid Ref SE0768 4904

Addingham

This was a healing well of the sore eyes kind. Stockinger Lane, an old lane from the village, leads up to Street Farm and the well which is a few yards from the Roman road from Ilkley. A section of Stockinger Lane is very attractive with dense hedges of holly, hazel and hawthorn. At the top of the lane the new main road needs to be crossed with care before walking across a field to Street Farm where there is a

Mill Ghyll Brook disappearing under Brook Street, Ilkley.

73

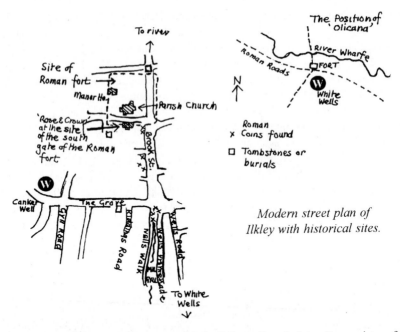

Modern street plan of Ilkley with historical sites.

stile. The well is hidden in the leafy little valley below. It consists of a concrete shaft 4 ft deep where clear water runs out of the sides to a shallow basin. There is a curved roof and a standing stone beside it. Logs of wood put there for safety partly obscure the well as does vegetation on the roof. It is surrounded by hawthorn.

WHITE WELLS

Grid Ref SE1181 4671

Ilkley

The waters of White Wells had been recognised as exceptional for a long time before it became a fashionable spa. A shepherd looking for lost sheep was said to be the one who discovered the well. He used the water for healing his leg. The original spring rose 'a furlong' (220 yards) above the present well house buildings, and was known before the 1700s. The water was brought down in stone pipes and came from more than one spring, each of a different quality. When laying pipes the foundations of the original well house was found, 7 yards by 5 yards and the spring was enclosed within a circular well with puddle cement at the back which forced the water to a higher level. The

Top: *The White Wells drinking fountain in the 1850s.*
Below: *The fountain today.*
Inset: *The author filling up a bottle.*

new well house was open to the sky originally and held two keyhole shaped baths.

In 1791 an advertisement was inserted in the *Leeds Intelligencer*.

Robert Dale of Ilkley takes this opportunity to inform the public that he is now fitting up two commodious new baths with sitting rooms adjoining for the accommodation of such persons as may wish to visit this Spaw. The medical qualities, famous for the cure of tumours and sores proceeding from scrophila and other disorders - recommended for - bad eyes - the spine - or the constitution enervated.

The well house was connected to a farm nearby and in 1819 improvements were made. To the west a 'Poor Bath' was built where lower charges were made (this is now the public toilets).

The quality of the water was described in the advertisement with great enthusiasm and detail, the main description of which states that it had a whitish look (is that why it is called White Wells?), clear, extremely cold, soft, medicinal and with the absence of particles. One person commented that it was so good that 'it is perhaps calculated to enter those minute vessels of the animal frame which are impervious to other fluids'. (In other words 'It reaches the parts which other waters cannot reach'!) and that 'a large quantity of the water may be drunk even immediately before dinner' without distending the stomach, giving a strong diuretic action.

William Middleton, the local land owning squire, was one of the originators of the development of the town as a spa and owned White Wells. In their heyday the wells had a full-time bathman. In about 1815 this position was occupied by William Butterfield. One midsummer morning he came to open the door but the key turned round in the lock. It seemed to melt. Eventually he managed to open the door and saw 'all over the water and dipping into it was a lot of little creatures dressed in green from head to foot, none of them more than eighteen inches high, and making a chatter and a jabber thoroughly unintelligible. They seemed to be taking a bath, only they bathed with all their clothes on. Soon however, one or two of them began to make off, bounding over the walls like squirrels. Finding they were all making ready for decamping, and wanting to have a word with them, he shouted at the top of his voice - indeed he declared afterwards he couldn't find anything else to say or do - "Hello there!". Then away the whole tribe went, helter skelter, toppling and tumbling, head over heels, heels over head, and all the while making a noise not unlike that of a disturbed nest of young partridges. The sight was so unusual, that he declared he either couldn't or daren't attempt to rush after them .... When the well had got quite clear of these

Top right: *White Wells showing the 'poor bath' on the right.*
Bottom left: *The carved stone spout in the bath.*
Bottom right: *The Eastern Bath in the early 1900s (now dry and hidden under floorboards).*

strange beings he ran to the door and looked to see where they had fled, but nothing was to be seen. He ran back into the bath to see if they had left anything behind; but there was nothing; the water lay still and clear just as he had left it the previous night.' (Smith *Fairies at Ilkley Wells*, 1898; Bord and Bord *Sacred Waters* 1985)

This description ties in with other accounts of meetings with fairies, little people, gentry, at old wells and other ancient features. Ilkley Moor (or Rombalds Moor) had more than its fair share of prehistoric remains. It is open to conjecture as to the nature of such beings and the claim of Mr Butterfield, but it does suggest that he experienced a different level of consciousness.

The fairies may have been evident at White Wells because by tradition they do not like 'their' wells to be Christianised. There is no suggestion that this well was ever considered to be 'holy', and even though the water was contained in a man-made building they did not seem to mind. The 'fountain' behind the building is still there. The water used to come freely out of a pipe and a cup was provided for drinking. Now there is only a gentle trickle obtained when a modern tap at the side is turned on.

Another account of the area includes the remark:- 'There was a rude circle of rocks on the reach behind White Wells 50 years ago' [1830] consisting of very large stones.' ('Walker' quoted in *Ilkley, Ancient and Modern*', Collyer and Turner, 1885). This is probably Blackstone Circle, a double stone circle recently rediscovered by Nigel Mortimer and confirmed by the West Yorkshire Archaeology Service.

There are rumours of other stone circles, strange occurrences and feelings, hauntings and legends of the fairy folk who, when the Saxons tried to build a church near White Wells, resented this and made it impossible to build, forcing them to build in the position of the present church.

CANKER WELL or SORE EYES WELL
Grid Ref SE1148 4763
Ilkley

This chalybeate well was probably discovered in the early days of the spa movement. Formerly called Pollards Well it lay 'in the fields beyond Green Lane Cottage' (Davies 1985). It was known for its healing properties in the 1880s. It is now situated at the north side of the Grove in a small public garden and consists of square stone plinth, feeder pipe and remains of a chain which held a drinking cup. It was erected in this form in 1923. It flows now only in very wet weather. It is on the line of the east-west Roman road.

Canker Well, Ilkley

Also in the garden is a stone trough taken from the first and most ambitious spa at Ben Rhydding. It was originally in a 'shrine' in the grounds, dedicated to the founder of the spa treatment system. The trough is beautifully carved with a lion spout at each end. The inscription on the side reads:-

In memory of Vinzenz Priessnitz The Silesian Peasant to whom the world is indebted for the blessing of the system of cure by Cole Water This fountain is gratefully erected and inscribed by Hamer Stansfield. Ben Rhydding. XXIX May MDCCXLIV

BEN RHYDDING HYDROTHERAPY ESTABLISHMENT

Grid Ref SE1360 4720

Ilkley

After White Wells was already established, cures by water (the Spa System) were revitalised by the above Silesian farmer in 1829. The system reached Britain and, in 1843, a wealthy businessman, Hamer Stansfield, and others made plans to bring the system to Ilkley because of the quality and quantity of the water supply. Treatment consisted of plunge baths, douche, hot air vapour, steam, Turkish baths, homeopathy, diet, exercise and games. Strict rules were also enforced.

In 1856 Wells House was built as a Hydro, closely followed by Craiglands, Troutbeck, the Grove, Rockwood and others. Their heyday was short-lived as they decline began in the 1880s for many and complex reasons. The huge establishments, wanting to retain customers, began to emphasise the holiday amenity of Ilkley, but the larger spas have now been demolished with the exception of Wells House, which is now part of Bradford and Ilkley Training College. Ben Rhydding Hydro site is now a housing estate.

One of the treatments of the Water Cure.

Ilkley Moor

The whole of Rombalds Moor between Ilkley and Bingley and between Menston and Silsden is a great watershed and contains many wells and springs. The moor abounds with prehistoric remains from earliest times to the Romans. The Bronze Age left the more numerous relics:- earthworks, stone circles and the mysterious cup and ring stone carvings. The waters, which must have attracted the people of the Bronze Age as well as those in the days of the spas, were of very differing consistencies in different parts of the moor. Some farmsteads rely today on the undiluted waters but there are many boreholes which are used for the general water supply, which has contributed to the reduction in the flow of many of the natural springs. As in other hilly areas, some residents swear by the purity of the water and take it neat while others use an ultra violet treatment system. According to some people, good quality water can be obtained from Horncliffe, Rivock, White, Silver, Hebers Ghyll Chalybeate, Low and Sweet Wells, but one must decide for oneself whether to risk the bacterial contamination from animals.

SILVER WELLS

Grid Ref SE1038 4674 and SE1045 4670
Ilkley Moor

There are two Silver Wells, both within the enclosure of Silver Well Cottage. They are called so after the silver sand which was seen at the bottom of the wells. Today they are both covered over by large stone slabs but the water can be heard trickling beneath. There are no other features near in the sheep grazed enclosure but birch and pine grow nearby. The waters were used until fairly recently and a local doctor had the utmost confidence in them when there was a drought elsewhere.

CHALYBEATE WELL, HEBER'S GHYLL

Grid Ref SE0990 4690
Ilkley Moor

This well was discovered in 1863 at the height of the spa fashion, providing medicinal water. Some say it flowed into Canker Well in Ilkley. It is situated in a beauty spot at the top of Hebers Ghyll. The water seeps out at the base of a curved wall west of Black Beck, which has a good flow of water. A few yards further down, the water flows into a trough. There has been recent restoration and in August 1993 the water trickled enough to wash tired and hot feet. The water is officially of drinking quality.

RIVOCK WELL

Grid Ref SE0776 4486
Ilkley Moor

Now within a conifer plantation, this well is below an old pond and it is to the north of the track running through the forest. There are cup and ring carvings nearby. Some say it has the sweetest of water.

SWEET WELL
Grid Ref SE1050 4421
Ilkley Moor

This well is high on the moor above East Morton. It is situated within 500 yards of the Roman road where an old cross marks a change in direction of the road. Sweet Well Dyke flows down to Sunnydale. In the 19th century shooting parties from Upwood House, further south on the Roman road, regularly gathered at the well in the grouse shooting season for luncheon. Its name is self-explanatory.

LOW WELL FENNY SHAW
Grid Ref SE1095 4225
Ilkley Moor

In a small wooded estate at the edge of the moor, at the junction of Heights Lane and Otley Road, this well (which is also said to have the sweetest of water) issues, then is directed under a track to flow into a duck pond before disappearing underground again. Todmor Stones ('tod' means fox; and so means 'the fox stones on the Morton boundary') lie to the north on the Morton parish boundary.

HORNCLIFFE WELL
Grid Ref SE1321 4331
Hawksworth

This well is just within the ancient boundary of Hawksworth, adjoining the Bingley parish boundary. It is on an old footpath across the moor from Baildon to Ilkley. There is a stone circle about 200 yards from the well to the north and the remains of a keeper's cottage by the well. In 1800 Joshua Briggs of Bingley and his wife came to live in the cottage to form a school. The well-known local poet, John Nicholson, was one of his pupils. Perhaps it is not strange that such an isolated and bleak place attracted Briggs and his followers. The very wild-

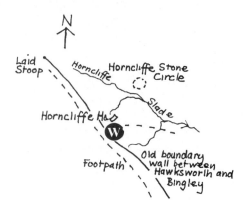

Horncliffe Well and gatepost to
Horncliffe House.

ness and the quality of the well water must have been attractive. The position of the building was nearly surrounded by streams and perhaps Briggs sensed the benefit of that as he lived there for twenty-seven years until his death.

Today a carved gatepost and stone rubble is all that can be seen of the cottage. The well is there and it contains good drinking water although it has been moved and modern repairs to water pipes, to provide drinking water elsewhere, have somewhat spoilt the surroundings.

BUBBLING WELL

Grid Ref SE2184 3801

Rawdon

In a field just north of a public footpath near to a Baptist chapel (now made into a house) is the Bubbling Well. The well was used for baptisms by the Baptists who originally they met under the Buckstone Rock in Crag Wood. Bubbling Well Wood, Wellroyd Wood and Wellroyd House lie to the north. The well is completely enclosed by a stone building, and locked. The keyholder is not known.

POPPLING WELL

Grid Ref SE1591 4860

Askwith

This is not now distinguishable from the stream called Poppling Well Beck, which runs through an overgrown, but cared for, attractive dell. There is no public access. A cup-marked rock lies 100 yards to the south at the base of a dead tree in the remnants of a hedge.

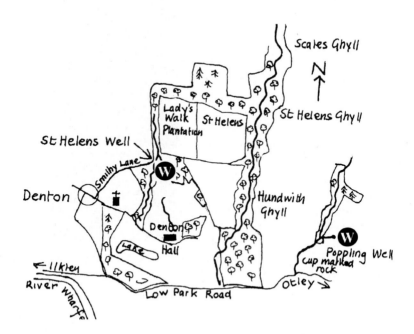

SKIRTFUL SPRING
Grid Ref SE1391 4423
Menston
This lies just within the ancient boundary of Menston in a very ancient part of Ilkley Moor. At the other side of the boundary are four tumuli, York Way (which was the Roman road), enclosures, Roms Law and other boundary stones, the Great Skirtful of Stones* and Grubstone Circle, a stone circle. The spring flows southwards to join Horncliffe Beck.

* Skirtful of Stones: This Bronze Age barrow was the subject of a local legend. The giant Rombald and his wife lived peacefully until one day when they had an argument. Rombald stormed off towards Almscliffe Cragg but his wife gathered stones in her apron to throw at him. The strings broke under the weight and they fell, forming Great and Little Skirtful of Stones.

HOG HILL WELL
Grid Ref SE1228 4300
Bingley
Now lost, this well used to lie by a medieval earthwork at the end of a long track from Graincliffe Reservoir, Otley Road. It is immediately north of West Spring (SE1220 4250). The area is best approached from the track at Dick Hudsons pub, which goes over Green Well Hill.

REDMANS SPA
Grid Ref SE1160 4342
Bingley
Sometimes marked as Richmonds Spa, it is near a public path from Micklethwaite Bank to Ilkley. It is a chalybeate well and named as a spa on OS maps.

COCKLAKE WELL
Grid Ref SE1376 4308
Hawksworth
On Cocklake Hill, this well lies south-west of an old boundary which goes through Horncliffe Well. The water flows into Horncliffe Beck near a footpath.

St Helen's Well House with Denton Hall in the background.

ST HELEN'S WELL or LADY'S WELL

Grid Ref SE1485 4920

Denton

Having easy access (see map page 84), this well is within an enclosed well house which may be 16th century. The square building, topped with a dome and ball finial, is built solidly of stone. There is a locked door to the interior. Inside is a shallow rectangular basin and the water is drinkable. Outside there is a small trough attached, having in it about one inch of water. A stream is diverted into the well and from there it is piped to Denton Hall and was at one time the only drinking water supply. The setting is in an attractive wooded part of Denton Hall Estate.

St Helen was the mother of Constantine the Great, and the reputed discoverer of 'the true cross'. She had many holy wells named after her. At Adel, Bramhope, Tadcaster and Burnsall are some of her holy wells in Yorkshire, with which county she is particularly associated. Place-names in the vicinity are St Helen's field, Lady's Walk Plantation, and St Helen's Ghyll, the latter being part of Hundwith Ghyll.

Elen, the pagan goddess, may have been associated with areas later given St Helen place-names. Scales Ghyll is also a name given to the upper part of the Ghyll (from the huts of the Scandinavian people) connecting the area with prechristian times.

Denton Hall, owned successively by the Fairfax, Ibbotson, Wycliffe families, and now owned by an electrical contractor, is the third building on the site. The others were destroyed by fire. There was a chapel of unknown antiquity which was demolished in 1778. The more recent church in the village is dedicated, not surprisingly, to St Helen.

BOOTS WELL

Grid Ref SE1871 4085

Otley/Weston

There are two springs which emerge here, near the boundary of Otley and Weston parishes. To the east lies Otley and to the west the village of Weston, with its old Hall and Banqueting House. There is no easy access but the wells are quite near the main road. They are in a lovely setting. The streams emerge, each from grassy and stony banks, around which hawthorn trees flourish. Dominating from above is an old oak, marked on maps as a boundary tree. On some older maps an ash is indicated north of the oak. In spring, violets and other spring flowers bloom amidst holly, elder and wild rose. The westernmost spring is fed to a cattle trough and the ground is muddy with the trampling feet of the cattle. The modern housing a field away is, hopefully, the very edge of any development.

SPA HILL WELL

Grid Ref SE006352

Oxenhope Moor

West of Leeshaw Reservoir is Spa Hill. In the wet area of the hillside beside the trees are three springs and the spa which gave its name to the hill. In the 19th century, local people celebrated Spa Sunday there, to reassert that the well was part of common land, and to make sure that it was still on their side of the boundary where Oxenhope Stoop stood.

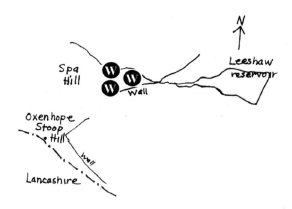

SLABBERING BABY WELL or OLD MAN'S MOUTH

Grid Ref SE2841 3981

Adel

Slabbering Baby, Adel.

Will someone unstop the gullet of the slabbering baby and restore the flow of air and water through it? Its mouth is big enough to fit a fist. At present the water flows through a crack in the stonework at the back of this unusually-shaped well. It is like a large bowl with a square rim tipped on its side. It is easy to find in Adel Wood on the Dalesway Meanwood Valley Trail where paths meet near a stream which runs down to the main beck. The well may be 18th or early 19th century. There is a suggestion of a garden with fruit trees nearby so there may have been a cottage here. The site is near to Adel Crags, the most prominent being two huge perched boulders. The wood is not far from the Norman church of St John the Baptist, which originally existed to serve the scattered communities of Airedale and Wharfedale, Adel village only coming into being in the 19th century. There are no significant trees over the well, but the alien Japanese Knotweed has gained a hold.

According to the *Yorkshire Post* of 21st September 1967 it is 'Where you can get at the freshest spring water in Leeds.' Today I'm not so sure of that.

YEADON

Grid Ref SE4120

Yeadon

The name Yeadon may have been derived from *ea* meaning 'water', and *don*, 'hill', - water on the hill. There is a large natural tarn here but the 'ea' was more likely to refer to the original well (now on Well Lane) and to the beck.

Illingworth wrote that in the 19th century there were seven wells in the town - at the Green (across from the Robin Hood pub, which changed its name to Tut N' Skive in 1993), Old Mill, Old Engine, Warm Lane, Swincar, Top of Henshaw, Albert Square and Moor Grange. There were also complaints then that rubbish was being deposited in the wells. Sounds familiar. A drinking fountain was erected for Queen Victoria's Jubilee at the junction of High Street and Victoria Avenue though later it was damaged.

All the wells have been filled in but today there is a move to restore some of them, beginning with the well on Well Lane.

Other Lost Wells

ALEGAR WELL
Grid Ref SE153227
Brighouse

Pronounced 'Elliker' or 'Holy Carr', it was 'a popular place of resort for young people on Palm Sunday mornings, when bottles of 'spanish juice' water were as numerous as the visitors' (Turner 1893). It was situated on the outskirts of Brighouse, by the Wakefield to Elland Road (A644), which was a turnpike road when Turner was writing. Alegar Bank Wood lies above the site. It was very near to the line of the Roman road which crossed the valley at that point.

Titus Salt offered to buy part of the Calder Valley from Brighouse Gasworks to Alegar Well in 1850, but he changed his mind and founded Saltaire instead.

ST HELEN'S WELL
Grid Ref SE213322 approx
Pudsey

A charter of 1260 mentions this well which was somewhere on the hillside, west of Fullneck. The name changed over the years into Sayntelling, an example of an oral tradition perpetuating the mishearing of the saint's name (see St Helen's Well, Denton, page 86).

JIM CRAVEN WELL
Grid Ref SE097328
Thornton.

In *Bronte Moors and Villages* by T Mackenzie, written in 1923, this well is described as being inhabited by the dreaded 'Guytrash'.

There is a path from Lower Kipping Lane (SE0975 3275) to Upper Headley, a medieval settlement, across the golf course over Bent Ing. This area was the haunt of Peggy wi't Lantern and Bloody Tongue (alias Guytrash). Peggy, a dame in a white cap entices unwary travellers to their door, with her lantern. Mackenzie writes: 'She was given to wandering, for they say to Jim Craven Well half a mile away, and it was a place to avoid after nightfall. The "Bloody Tongue" was a great dog with red eyes and a huge tail. When he drank from the beck [Pinchbeck?] the water ran red right past the bridge down nearly to Bradford. As soon as it was dark he would lope up to the narrow flagged causeway to the cottage at the top of Bent Ing [Lower Kipping Lane?] giving a deep bark. . . . We used to sit [to look out for the dog] in the filled in pit which makes a hump in the middle of the field [still there] - only one girl saw him. A girl who lived at Headley had to go back home one night alone - her friends dare not go with her. They reached the end of the passage leading to the fields and gazed into the black well where Bloody Tongue resides but could go no further'.

The position of the well is very unclear from the above - at the end of the passage or half a mile away, but it is a rather spooky tale with similarities to other descriptions of haunted wells.

Green Well
Grid Ref SE2132
Pudsey

Rayner in *History of Pudsey* says that during Beltane (May Day) water was carried to and from this well in tritual and profane use. It was of refreshing quality and good humour. Maypole dancing took place nearby. The whole area has now been built up and the green lost.

There are many more wells which have not been researched. Some of these are:
Jacob's Well, Rodley
Acre Well, Pudsey
Petrifying Well, Shelf
Rake Holes Well, Shelf
Annett Hole Well, Shelf
Holycroft, Exleyhead, Keighley
Lady Well, Micklethwaite

I invite anyone who has additional information about wells, epecially those having a specific name, to contact the author c/o Heart of Albion Press, 2 Cross Hill Close, Wymeswold, Loughborough, LE12 6UJ

Ley line passing through or near old sites and natural features.

Distance 15 miles. Most points lie within 200 yards. There are two wells on the line, Horncliffe Well and Bolling Hall Well.

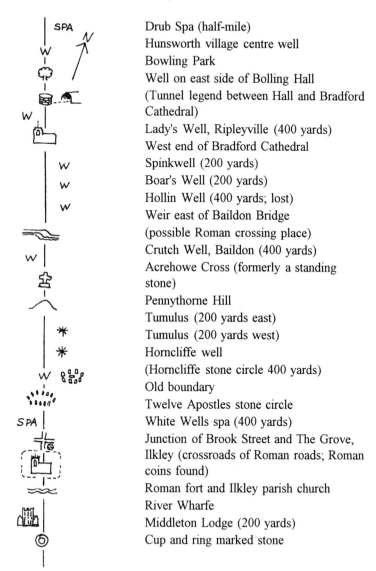

Drub Spa (half-mile)
Hunsworth village centre well
Bowling Park
Well on east side of Bolling Hall
(Tunnel legend between Hall and Bradford Cathedral)
Lady's Well, Ripleyville (400 yards)
West end of Bradford Cathedral
Spinkwell (200 yards)
Boar's Well (200 yards)
Hollin Well (400 yards; lost)
Weir east of Baildon Bridge
(possible Roman crossing place)
Crutch Well, Baildon (400 yards)
Acrehowe Cross (formerly a standing stone)
Pennythorne Hill
Tumulus (200 yards east)
Tumulus (200 yards west)
Horncliffe well
(Horncliffe stone circle 400 yards)
Old boundary
Twelve Apostles stone circle
White Wells spa (400 yards)
Junction of Brook Street and The Grove, Ilkley (crossroads of Roman roads; Roman coins found)
Roman fort and Ilkley parish church
River Wharfe
Middleton Lodge (200 yards)
Cup and ring marked stone

Glossary

CHALYBEATE WELL

Pronounced 'kal-i-be-at'. A water source containing iron salts which leave a red deposit if concentrated enough. Valued for its medicinal qualities.

CLOSE

Private property usually enclosed. A field.

CUP AND RING MARKED ROCKS

Probably Bronze Age rock carvings in the form of circular depressions, some with carved rings around them. There are other carvings of the same date which are more elaborate, all for an unknown purpose.

DOWSING

A means of detecting underground water and otherwise imperceptible objects or unseen energies by the movement of a rod or pendulum held in the hand.

GABBLERATCHETS

See GUYTRASH

GUYTRASH

Dragons, sea serpents, devils, hobs, fairies, white women, large cats, kangaroos, strange lights, flying saucers and black dogs called Guytrashes: all these have been seen and recorded throughout the centuries in Britain, down to the present day, none of them leaving any physical remains. Many of these phenomena are associated with wells. People who fall into wells and are killed turn into ghosts. Peoples' worst fears are enacted on dark nights, especially if they are going home from the pub, and some manifestations just come 'out of the blue'.

It seems that such non-physical entities and people's strong thought forms sometimes coincide at specific locations; places with long associations with human habitation and especially near water. Other manifestations occur where there has been a human tragedy, or just before a death.

The Guytrash takes the form of a large shaggy dog with broad, webbed feet. It has drooping 'saucer' eyes and walks with a splashing sound (the 'trash' sound of old fashioned boots). The Guytrash is related to the spectral hounds of Gabriel, Gabriels Ratchets, which make a gabbling sound as they chase across the sky, hence the local term 'Gabbleratchets'.

Gabbleratchets were seen circling Idle Hill and the Guytrash followed three frightened men along Bradford Road near Nooking Well. It was also seen disappearing in Jim Craven Well, Thornton. In Baildon it was seen near to Binns Well and the Holy Well at Halliwell Banks. It was noticed in other parts of Bradford too until gaslight began to light the streets. Its appearance is not recorded after that, for who is afraid of ghosts when it is light?

LEY LINES

First named by Alfred Watkins in the 1920s, they are described as an invisible line connecting significant points in the landscape of ancient origin, such as wells, hills, clumps of trees, earthworks etc. There is much speculation as to whether ley lines exist; whether they are some kind of unseen energy or ancient paths.

PARKIN PIGS

The baking of Parkin Pigs derives from a Scandinavian tradition. Speight says that at every autumn fair in October, school children from Bingley eat Parkin Pigs. They are an image of the solar diety, the sacred boar, a representative of both the Norse god Freyr and his consort Freya, who were associated with autumn festivals. There was an old custom throughout Britain of presenting a Boars Head with an apple in its mouth at the dining table at special feasts, especially at Christmas. St Antony was a protector of animals and his emblem was a boar.

PIN STONE

A stone placed near a holy well in which there was a depression full of water. Pins were placed in the water as an offering.

PIN WELL OR PEN WELL

Pin wells were holy or healing wells where pins were deposited to the residing spirit, diety or saint as an offering for the waters in return for healing or to grant a wish. Pins were usually bent, probably as part of the sacrifice of the object. In Roman times, gold 'pins' and other jewellery were deposited in wells, the pins being of much higher value than they are for us today, so that any offering was not done lightly.

RAG WELL

A holy well where it was the custom for the gift of the water to be recognised by an offering in the form of rags which were tied onto the overhanging trees. The tradition was that as the rags rotted the disease was cured. This custom is still practised in some areas but mistakes of using non-rotting synthetic fabrics and paper tissues have confounded the tradition. In some areas the rotting rags were called 'memaws'.

STOOP
A boundary stone or a large significant standing stone.

TUMULUS
An ancient burial mound of earth which is usually dated Bronze Age (approximately 3,000 to 1,500 BC).

WART STONE
A stone with a carved depression which held water. The hand was placed in the water to cure warts. The mineral properties in the stone probably gave the water healing qualities.

References and Bibliography

GENERAL

Up-to-date publications on wells are few, may of them on a county basis. Nationally, *Sacred waters* by Janet and Colin Bord is the most comprehensive but gives details of only three holy wells in West Yorkshire.

Janet and Colin Bord *Sacred Waters* Granada 1985

J C Cooper *An illustrated encyclopaedia of traditional symbols* Thames and Hudson 1978

Paul Devereux *Places of Power* Blandford 1990

Robert C Hope *Legendary Lore of the Holy Wells of England* Elliot Stock, 1893

R. Merrifield *The archaeology of ritual and magic* Batsford 1987

Nigel Pennick *Earth Harmony* 1987

Crichton Porteous *The Well Dressing Guide* Derbyshire Countryside Ltd 1973

G Target *Holy Ground* Bishopgate Press 1971

Bob Trubshaw *Holy Wells and Springs of Leicestershire and Rutland* Heart of Albion Press 1990

Cumming Walters *Holy Wells* Originally published 1898, reprinted Heart of Albion Press 1991.

YORKSHIRE

T Allen *History of the County of York* Vol.5 1831

H Armitage *Halifax Antiquary* 1969

F Barratt *A History of Queensbury* Queensbury Centenary Celebrations Committee 1963

M L Baumber *A Pennine Community on the Eve of the Industrial Revolution Keighley and Haworth 1660-1700* M.L. Baumber c.1975

J H Bell 'Some Fragments of Local Medical History' from *Journal of Bradford Historical and Antiquarian Society 1881-1895 part 2* 1892

Joseph Bentley *Illustrated Handbook of the Bradford City Parks* Parks and Cemeteries Committee 1926

Edmond Bogg *The Old Kingdom of Elmet* 1902

Dorothy Burrows *Bingley A Look at the Past* D. Burrows 1985

David Carpenter *Ilkley. The Victorian Era* Smith Settle 1986

R Collyer and J Horsefall Turner *Ilkley ancient and modern* William Walker and Sons 1885

E T Cowling *Rombalds Way* William Walker 1946

Crabtree *Shipley Through the Camera* 1902 Reprint of W Peel privately circulated work 1857

William Cudworth *Round About Bradford* First published 1876, reprinted as 2 vols Mountain Press 1968

William Cudworth *Rambles Round Horton* Thos. Brear & Co 1886

William Cudworth *History of Bolton and Bowling* Thos. Brear & Co 1891

William Cudworth *History of Manningham, Heaton and Allerton* W Cudworth 1896

William Cudworth *History of Bolton in Bradford Dale* 1927

Keith Davis *Ilkley in Old Picture Postcards* European Library (Netherlands) 1985

J.H. Dixon *Chronicles and Stories of the Craven Dales* Simpkin Marshall 1881

E E Dodd *Bingley. A Yorkshire Town Through Nine Centuries* M T D Rigg 1958

E E Dodd *History of Bingley Grammar School* Lund and Humphreys 1930

M.L. Faull and S.A. Moorhouse (editors) *West Yorkshire: an Archaeological Survey* Series of maps to AD1500 West Yorkshire MCC 4 vols 1981

C F Foreshaw (editor) *Yorkshire Notes and Queries* Vol 2 , 1906

Elsie M Fletcher *The Story of Menston* Menston 1953

Lucy Gill *Baildon memories* M T D Rigg 1986

Sydney Greenbank *Druids Altar* 1929

T W Hanson 'Two Northowram Homesteads ' in *Bradford Antiquary* Vol XI 1887 republished S R Publishing 1968

T W Hanson *The Story of Old Halifax* King 1920

J A Hegginbottom 'Early Christian Sites in Calderdale ' in *Halifax Antiquary* 1988

David Hey *Yorkshire from AD1000* Longmans 1986

T Illingworth *Yeadon, Yorkshire* T Illingworth 1972; reprinted 1980

Sidney Jackson *Celtic and other stone heads* S. Jackson 1973

John James *History and Topography of Bradford* 1841, reprinted 1967

John James *History of Bradford and its Parishes* Didsbury 1866; reprinted Mountain Press 1977 as 3 vols

William Keighley *Keighley Past and Present* Arthur Hall 1879

A Laurence *A history of Menston and Hawksworth* Smith Settle 1991

T Mackenzie *Bronte Moors and Villages* 1923

D Stuart Metcalfe *Around Farsley and Calverley in times past* Countryside Publications 1981

John La Page *The story of Baildon* J La Page 1951

Charles Ogden *History of Bradford* Cheltenham 1929

Charles Ogden 'Bradford in the Olden Times' from *History of Bradford* 1890

James Parker *Great Horton in Bye-gone Days* J Feather and Son 1900

James Parker *Clayton, Old Dolphin etc.* J Parker 1901

James Parker *Illustrated history of Wibsey, Low Moor, etc,* J Feather and Son 1902

James Parker *Illustrated History from Hipperholme to Tong* Lund Humphreys 1904

F.R. Pearson *Romans in Yorkshire* Brown 1936

Guy Raglan Philips 'Carved heads and lead figurines' *The Dalesman* Vol. 33 1971/2

Guy Raglan Philips 'Well shrines of ancient pagan faith must not vanish' *The Dalesman* Vo.34 1972/3

W E Preston 'Some Local Holy Wells ' in *Bradford Antiquary* vol. 7, 1933

Simeon Rayner *History of Pudsey* Longmans Green and Co 1887, reprinted M T D Rigg 1986

G F Renton *Water supply of Bradford* unpublished. Copy in West Yorkshire Archives, Bradford

Martin Rigg *Round About Aireborough* M T D Rigg 1988

Martin Rigg *An Aireborough selection* M T D Rigg 1991

Andy Roberts *Ghosts and Legends of Yorkshire* Jarrold 1992

Wilfred Robertshaw 'The Township of Manningham in the 17th century ' from *Bradford Antiquary* Part 27 Vol 6 1935

Wilfred Robertshaw 'The Lost Hamlet of Cockham ' in *Bradford Antiquary* Vol 6 1938

'S' 'There's romance at the bottom of a well', *The Dalesman* Vol. 19 1957/8

A E Smith *Place Names of the West Riding* English Place-name Society 1961

Andrea N Smith *Holy Wells in and around Leeds Bradford and Pontefract* Unpublished thesis 1981. Copy in West Yorkshire Archaeology Service, Wakefield

Charles C Smith 'Fairies at Ilkley Wells ' *Folklore Record* Vol 1 1898

Harry Speight *Chronicles and Stories of Old Bingley* 1897; reprinted as *Bingley and District* Elliot Stock 1904

Harry Speight *Pleasant Walks Around Bradford* 1890

Harry Speight *Upper Wharfedale* Elliot Stock 1900, reprinted Smith Settle 1988

Marion Taylor *A short history of Baildon* Bradford Libraries 1987

Horsfall Turner *Haworth Past and Present* J S Jowett 1879; reprinted Olicana Books 1971

Horsfall Turner *Ancient Bingley* H Turner1897

Horsfall Turner *A Springtime Saunter* 3rd edn Halifax Courier Ltd 1913; reprinted M T D Rigg 1986

Wright Watson *Idlethorpe* Idlethorpe Publication Committee 1950

Edna Whelan and Ian Taylor *Yorkshire Holy Wells and Sacred Springs* Northern Lights 1989

Rob Wilson *Holy wells and spas of South Yorkshire* R. Wilson 1991

Wright *Wright's Antiquities of Halifax* 1738, reprint by Horsfall Turner

Index

Abbey Well, Norr   48
Acre Well, Baildon   42
Acre Well, Pudsey   90
Acrehowe Cross   92
Addingham well   73
Adel well   88
Ailsa Well, Bingley   16-19
Albert Square fountain,
        Queensbury   70
Albert Square Well, Yeadon   88
Alders Well, Hawksworth   53
Alegar Well, Brighouse   89
Ambler Thorn Well,
        Queensbury   69
Annett Hole Well, Shelf   90
Ashwell, Heaton   13
Ashwell, Manningham   12
Askwith well   84

Baildon wells   41-47, 54
Bairstow's Pump, Queensbury   70
Barkhill Well, Idle   33
Barrel Well, Wibsey   35
Bath Well, Horton   11
Bay of Biscay well   37
Bell Bank Well, Bingley   22
Beldon Hill Well, Great Horton 69
Ben Rhydding Hydrotherapy
        Establishment, Ilkley   79-80
Bingley wells   15-22, 38-39, 85
Binnswell, Baildon   42
Birkin Well, Hawksworth   53
Blackey House well, Marley   23
Boar's Well, Bradford4, 6, 13, 925

Bobbling Well, Baildon   46
Bolling Hall Wells,
        Bradford   10, 92
Booth's Pumps, Queensbury   70
Boots Well, Otley/Weston   87
Boundary Place Pump,
        Queensbury   70
Bowling wells   10
Bradford wells   4-15
Brickfield Pump, Queensbury   70
Brighouse well   89
Broomfield Well, Queensbury   70
Brown Hill Well, Bingley   22
Bubbling Well, Rawdon   84
Burnsall well   1
Burnwells, Idle   33-5

Calverley wells   55-59
Canker Well, Ilkley   73, 74, 78
Catherine Slack Well,
        Queensbury   70
Catstone Well, Harden   49
Chalybeate well, Heber's Ghyll,
        Ilkley   81
Chellow Wells, Chellow Grange 38
Claremont Farm Well, Norr   49
Clayton wells   35-6, 70
Cloven Hoof Well,
        Shipley Glen   26
Cockham (or Cockin) wells,
        Clayton   70
Cocklake Well, Hawksworth   85
Coldspring, Cullingworth   39
Coldwell, Harecroft   39
Coley Hall well   66
Cottingley wells   40
Crag Well, Baildon   41

Crag Well, Shipley 26-7
Crossley Hall wells, Bradford 11
Cruckleswells, Bradford 6, 8
Crutch Well, Baildon 42, 92
Cullingworth well 39
Cup and ring marked
    stones 81, 84, 92, 93
Currer Laithe well, Bingley 23

Dakwell, Cockham 71
Dora Well, Bowling 10
Drighlington well 62
Drub Spa 64, 92
Druids Altar, Bingley 23
Druids Well, Bingley 24
Ducking Well, Haworth 49

Eaglands Well, Baildon 45
Early or Hurley Stone, Baildon 42
East Bierley village well 61
Elm Crag Well, Bingley 22
Emsley's Pump, Queensbury 70

Fairies 21, 42, 63, 78
Fairy Well, Gilstead 21
Fairy Well, Roberttown 63
Far Well, Baildon 44
Farewell, Calverley 57
Flappit Spring 41
Franks Well, Baildon 45

Gabbleratchets 93
Gilstead, Fairy Well 21
Goff Well, Keighley 24
Granby Pump, Queensbury 70
Great Horton wells 69
Green Well, Pudsey 90

Griff Well, Wyke 61
Guiseley wells 54-5
Guytrash 90, 93

Halifax wells 64-68
Harden wells 47-49
Harecroft well 39
Hartley Well Spring,
    Bay of Biscay 37
Hartshead well 62
Hawksworth wells 53-54, 82-83, 85
Healy Well Oak, Drighlington 62
Heaton wells 13, 89
Heber's Ghyll well 81
Helliwell Banks Well, Baildon 45
Helliwell Syke Well,
    Priestley Green 65
Hill Top Well, Queensbury 70
Hog Hill Well, Bingley 85
Hollingwood Lane Well,
    Great Horton 69
Hollin Well, Bradford 92
Holts Well, Clayton 36
Holy Well, Eccleshall 29
Holy Well, Halifax 67, 68
Holy Well, Priestley Green 64
Holycroft, Exleyhead 90
Holywell Ash, Manningham 13, 15
Horncliffe stone circle 82, 92
Horncliffe Well,
    Hawksworth 82-83, 92
Horton wells 11
Hungerhill Pump, Queensbury 70
Hunsworth village centre well 92
Hurley or Early Stone, Baildon 42
Hurstwells, Clayton 71
Hydrotherapy 79-80

Idle wells 30-35
Ilkley wells 72-82
Ing Well, Wyke 61

Jacky Well, Great Horton 69
Jacob's Well, Bradford 5
Jacob's Well, Rodley 90
Janet's or Jennet's Well, Bingley 21
Jennet's Well, Keighley 50, 52
Jer Loine Well, Great Horton 69
Jerusalem Farm Wells, Thornton 37
Jim Craven Well, Thornton 89
Joe's Well, Baildon 41
Jonas Well, Halifax 67, 68
Judson Well, Shipley 26
Jumbles Well, Pudsey 60

Keighley wells 24, 50, 52, 90
Kirk Well, Bowling 10
Knowles Pump, Queensbury 70

Lady Well, Hartshead 62
Lady Well, Menston 57
Lady Well, Micklethwaite 90
Lady's Well, Bowling 9, 10
Laycock well 50
Ley lines 92, 94
Loin or Loyn Spaht, Baildon 43-5
Listers Well, Priestley Green 64
Low Well Fenny Shaw, Ilkley 82
Low Well, Clayton 35
Low Well, Idle 31
Low Well, Shipley 28

Manningham wells 12-14
Manuels, Bingley 38
Manywells Spring, Bingley 38

Marley Brow wells 23
Menston wells 57, 85
Merwell, Clayton 71
Micklethwaite well 90
Mitton Spring, Baildon 47
Mitton Spring, Shipley 26
Moor Close Lane Bottom Well,
    Queensbury 69
Moor Grange Well, Yeadon 88
Moorhead Well, Cullingworth 39
Moorside wells, Baildon 46

Near Well, Baildon 45
New House Farm Well,
    Queensbury 70
Newsholme well 50
Nooking Well, Idle 33
Norr wells 48, 49
Northowram well 55
Nursery Well, Shipley Glen 26-7

Old Engine Well, Yeadon 88
Old Hall Well, Cottingley 40
Old Ike Well, Baildon 46-7
Old Man's Mouth, Adel 88
Old Mill Well, Yeadon 90
Old Road Well, Great Horton 69
Olicana (Roman fort) 72
Otley well 87
Our Lady's Well, Bingley 22

Parkin pigs 47, 94
Patchett's Pump, Queensbury 70
Peggy Well, Riddlesden 52
Petrifying Well, Shelf 90
Pin Stone, Manningham 14
Pin stones 94
Pin wells 8, 94

Pollards Well 78
Poppling Well, Askwith 84
Priestley Green wells 64-65
Priestthorpe Spring, Bingley 21
Prince of Wales Park well,
        Bingley 20
Pudsey wells 59-60, 89, 90, 94

Queensbury wells 69-70

Rag wells 94
Rake Holes, Shelf 90
Randall Well, Bradford 7
Rawdon well 84
Raygate Well, Shipley 26
Redmans Spa, Bingley 85
Riddlesden well 52
Rivock Well, Ilkley 81
Roberttown well 63
Rodley well 90
Romboulds Moor 80
Roper Lane Well, Queensbury 69
Royd Field Farm well, Bingley 23

Salt, Titus 89
Sandals Pond 44
Scarlet Height Well,
        Queensbury 70
Schoolhouse Well, Bradford 8
Seth Spring, Bingley 38
Sharket Head Well, Queensbury 70
Shelf wells 90
Shibden Head Well, Queensbury 70
Shipley Glen wells 25-28
Silver Wells, Ilkley 81
Skirtful of Stones 85
Skirtful Spring, Menston 85

Slabbering Baby Well, Adel 88
Smale Well, Pudsey 59
Sore Eyes Well, Shipley 25-6, 78
Sour Heads Well, Queensbury 70
Spa Hill Well, Oxenhope 87
Spa Well, Bingley 19, 23
Spinkwell, Bradford 5, 6, 9, 13
Spring Head Well,
        Great Horton 69
Spring Head Well, Queensbury 70
St Anthony's Well, Northowram 55
St Antony's Well, Harden 47
St Helen's Well, Denton 84, 86-87
St Helen's Well, Pudsey 89
St Ives Well, Harden 47
St John the Baptist's Well,
        Halifax 67
St John's Well, Coley Hall 66
Stone circles 85, 92
Stone heads near wells 20, 46
Stoop 95
Storr Hill Well, Addingham 73
Sugar Well, Great Horton 69
Sunnybank Well, Baildon 54
Swamp Well, Queensbury 70
Sweet Well, Ilkley 82
Sweet Willy Well, Wrose 28
Swincar Well, Yeadon 88

Tea Well, Horton 11
Temperance Movement 20
Tentercroft well 44
Thor's Well, Burnsall 1
Thornton wells 36-7, 90
Thwaites Brow wells 23
Tombling Well, Calverley 55
Tong Well, Tong 59

Top of Henshaw Well, Yeadon 88
Town End Well, Great Horton 69
Town Well (Upper and Lower),
      Idle 31
Town Wells, Calverley 56
Town Wells, Cottingley 40
Trough Field Well,
      Great Horton 69
True Well, Newsholme 50, 53
Turnwell, Clayton 71
Twelve Apostles stone circle 92

Union Well, Great Horton 69

Village Well, East Bierley 61

Walker Lane Well, Queensbury 70
Warm lane Well, Yeadon 88
Wart Stone, Manningham 13, 14
Wart stones 95

Watering Well, Bingley 15
Well Croft, Shipley 28
Well Heads, Thornton 36
Well on the Green, Idle 33
Well opposite Alexandra Inn, Idle 31
Well Spring, Idle 32
West Wood Well, Calverley 58
Weston well 87
Wheatcroft Well, Wyke 61
White Well, Harden 48
White Wells, Ilkley 74-78, 92
Wibsey well 35
William a Royd's Well, Idle 30, 32
Wilsden well 48-49
Wood Well, Shipley 26-7
Workhouse Well, Horton 11
Wyke wells 61

Yeadon wells 88

Forthcoming Summer 1994:

A guide to the
CIRCLES, STANDING STONES
and
LEGENDARY ROCKS
of the
WEST RIDING
YORKSHIRE

Paul Bennett

£3.50 plus 40 p p&p

Send s.a.e. for full catalogue.

HEART OF ALBION PRESS
2 Cross Hill Close, Wymeswold
Loughborough, LE12 6UJ